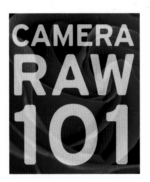

CAMERA RAW 101

Better Photos with Photoshop, Elements, and Lightroom

JON CANFIELD

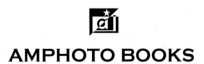

AMPHOTO BOOKS

AN IMPRINT OF WATSON-GUPTILL PUBLICATIONS
NEW YORK

www.amphotobooks.com
www.crownpublishing.com
www.watsonguptill.com

Library of Congress Control Number: 2009920540

ISBN 978-0-8174-3229-4

Senior Editor: Julie Mazur
Project Editor: Carrie Cantor
Production Director: Alyn Evans
Art Director: Jess Morphew
Design by Jan Derevjanik

1 2 3 4 5 6 7 8 / 16 15 14 13 12 11 10 9

First Edition

Printed in Singapore

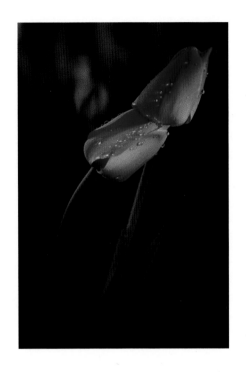

TO KATHY,

my wonderful wife and best friend

CONTENTS

FOREWORD

Sometimes it seems like giving good advice is remarkably easy. Just offer the conservative recommendation, and you're pretty safe. This certainly holds true when offering photographic advice. Use a tripod. Use mirror lockup. Use a cable release. And of course, digital cameras have provided us with the latest addition to the long list of "safe" recommendations for photographers: Capture in RAW. The common thread among all these, of course, is that if you follow the recommendations you'll achieve images of higher technical quality on a more consistent basis.

The problem is, while most photographers can very easily set their digital cameras to capture in RAW, they don't understand how to best deal with those RAW captures to achieve their ultimate goal: producing the best images possible.

Fortunately, you hold in your hands the solution to this problem. Jon Canfield has written an excellent book that—in plain English—explains everything you need to know to make the most of RAW capture after the picture has been taken. In addition to detailed coverage of how to convert your RAW images with both basic and advanced techniques, Jon shows you how to download the images, get them organized, and then put the finishing touches on your RAW captures after conversion to get them ready for printing. He even demonstrates how you can automate the process of converting a large number of RAW captures quickly and easily when speed is your primary objective.

RAW capture enables photographers to exercise unprecedented control over their images, and I think that is a truly exciting thing. For many photographers, working in a wet darkroom wasn't an attractive option, so they gave up much of the control over the final interpretation of their image. The digital darkroom has enabled photographers to have that control again (and so much more!), all in the comfort of their computer chairs. But RAW takes this control far beyond what was possible before. With it, we can now fine-tune the color temperature, extract maximum detail from shadow and highlight areas, and work with confidence using high-bit data to ensure the best quality possible in the final result, and Jon will guide you through all these topics in this book.

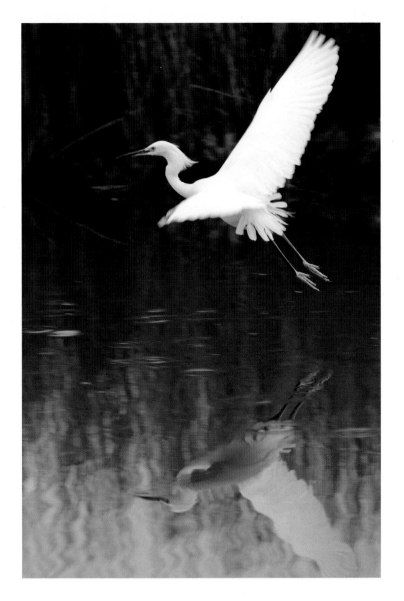

I think most photographers have become familiar with the concept that RAW capture can help them achieve the best quality possible. With this book, you'll go beyond the theory and learn to process your RAW captures with skill and confidence. And if you had any concerns about the complexities involved with RAW capture, let me put your mind at ease. I am fortunate enough to know Jon personally, and I can tell you that reading this book is just like having a conversation with him over lunch: comfortable and educational. You're in for a treat, and you'll be amazed at how much better your images can really be!

—TIM GREY, photographer, teacher, and author
or coauthor of fifteen books on digital imaging

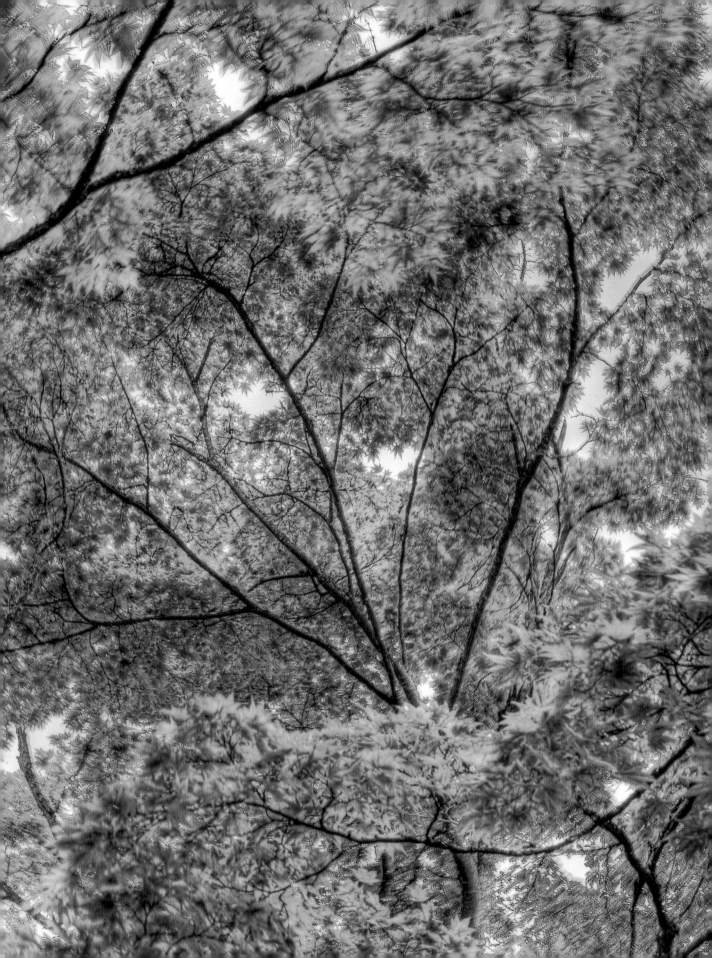

INTRODUCTION

This book is for any digital photographer who is interested in going beyond the preset options in the camera and is ready to take control over the creative process. If you have read about RAW capture, or tried it yourself and ran into the roadblocks most of us did at the start, this book is all about giving you the information you need to make RAW work for you. You don't need to be a Photoshop Elements or Photoshop expert. In fact, if you have basic familiarity with either of these programs, you're ready to go. All you really need is a camera that captures RAW files and a copy of Elements or Photoshop with Camera Raw.

WHAT IS RAW?

A RAW file is the digital equivalent of a film negative. As with film, the RAW file contains information on the amount of light that was seen by the sensor. It knows nothing of how you intended the scene to be captured or of what lighting was used. You retain the control over how the RAW file is processed just as you did with a film negative.

Every digital capture begins as a RAW file, but when you select JPEG as the output, the camera's built-in RAW converter processes the file, applying the white balance, color correction, and compression settings according to the camera settings. It also converts your file to 8 bit, throwing out a good deal of color information that can be used for more control when editing the image.

In its most basic form, a RAW file is simply a collection of the luminance values recorded at each photo site at the time of capture, along with data containing the camera settings and most likely a JPEG thumbnail that is used for review on the camera LCD.

Although RAW files are technically just the recorded value of light from each photo site, every camera manufacturer interprets this data differently, even when the same imaging sensor is used. This has led to the proliferation of RAW conversion programs—from independent companies as well as each of the camera manufacturers. The most popular option for many, though, and the subject of this book, is Adobe Camera Raw, found in Photoshop Elements, CS4, and Lightroom.

There are ongoing talks of standardizing the RAW format, but the chances of this happening in the foreseeable future are slim at best. With Adobe's creation and release of DNG specification, or digital negative, there is an increased likelihood that standards may become a reality.

A key advantage to the DNG format, aside from Adobe's influence in the digital imaging market, is that your RAW files will be convertible in the future. Thus, you're covered in the event that you replace your digital camera with a different brand or find that support for your camera's RAW format has been discontinued.

WHY YOU SHOULD SHOOT RAW

When total control and the highest possible image quality are needed, RAW is the perfect format to use. The greater dynamic range, color depth, and post-capture editing capabilities make the RAW format the best choice in most situations.

RAW files shouldn't be seen as the lazy person's way to great images, though. A poorly composed image, an out-of-focus image, or one with gross exposure errors isn't going to be magically transformed into a quality photograph because you were able to edit the RAW file. It's still the responsibility of the photographer to capture the best possible image *at the time of capture*.

ADVANTAGES OVER JPEG AND TIFF

RAW files free the photographer from having to be satisfied with what the camera thinks are the correct values for sharpening, noise reduction, and white balance. The differences can be startling! Since this information is all stored in addition to the file, it becomes possible to make changes to them after the fact. This is where the RAW format becomes so valuable.

When shooting in JPEG, the camera processes the color values based on the current white balance setting in the camera to create a final image. The file is then compressed to save space using the current quality setting in the camera. RAW capture, on the other hand, does no color interpretation in-camera but depends on the RAW converter software to handle this task. Hence, you have much more freedom after the capture to either fine-tune the image or make corrections to basic problems such as improperly set white balance.

RAW is the only capture method that preserves the full color fidelity of the image. With JPEG, you immediately throw away one third of the color information in your image. The sensor in most cameras records data as a 12- or 14-bit file, giving each pixel one of 4,096 levels or more of color. To take advantage of this, you'll need to shoot in RAW mode. JPEG only supports 8 bits per pixel, reducing the possible colors to 256 per pixel. It's easy to see that you'll record a more accurate representation of the subject with at least 4,096 choices than with 256! Less color information means that you have less latitude when editing the image for final output.

JPEG is a lossy compression method. Every time a file is saved in the JPEG format it loses a little more fidelity.

JPEG and TIFF also apply sharpening and noise reduction at the time of capture. If you've set these incorrectly and don't catch the error, you have little choice in the edit phase. I strongly feel that the camera does not know what my intended use for an image is and should never be allowed to choose the sharpening or noise reduction it "thinks" I want.

Saving in camera as TIFF is becoming much less common in recent cameras. Although some, such as the Canon D-SLRs, actually tag their RAW files as TIFF, these are not true TIFF files. TIFF, or Tagged Image File Format, is a standard file type for bitmap, or raster, data. Unlike JPEGs, TIFFs are not subject to lossy compression or to only 8 bits of color information. The file sizes are large; a 16-bit TIFF file will be about three times the size of the same RAW file, because TIFF is saved at 16 bits rather than the 12 to 14 bits recorded by the camera. The extra bit depth is an advantage over JPEG, but the same control issues that JPEG suffers from are present in TIFF capture as well. Color balance, sharpening, and noise reduction are all applied directly to the image at the time of capture. The only advantage that TIFF offers over JPEG is color fidelity and lossless compression. To be honest, I can't think of a single instance where saving as a TIFF file in camera is a good option.

WHEN RAW ISN'T THE BEST CHOICE

There are times when the extra work involved with RAW processing can't be justified. As an example, photojournalists will typically shoot in JPEG when shooting for assignments. The image files are smaller, important for quick transfer to the newsroom, and the JPEGs can be used with little or no extra work before publishing. Another time when JPEG may be a better choice is when you are shooting youth sports events and want to make prints for sale right at the site. This is another case of speed being more important than ultimate quality.

ELEMENTS, PHOTOSHOP, OR LIGHTROOM: WHICH IS RIGHT FOR YOU?

This book uses Adobe Camera Raw, which comes in three flavors. The first two—Photoshop Elements (Elements 6 on Macintosh, Elements 7 on Windows) and Photoshop CS4—are very similar. The version of Camera Raw included with Elements is based on the one included with Photoshop CS. Some advanced features have been removed, but all of the essentials are there.

Photoshop CS4 has a whole new version of Camera Raw that, while keeping the same basic interface, has added features to make it more capable than ever, especially for batch processing and advanced exposure correction.

Finally, there is Adobe Lightroom 2.1. This is a new application that is built just for photographers and has a self-contained approach to image management and editing that many will find appealing. The RAW conversion controls in Lightroom are identical to those in Photoshop CS4. The table opposite shows the major feature differences between the two versions of Camera Raw.

So which one should you use? The answer is simpler than you might expect. If you are just getting started with digital imaging, I recommend starting out with Photoshop Elements. Not only does it include most of the functionality of Photoshop CS4, but it does it with an interface that is easier to use and learn and at a much better price.

If you already own Photoshop CS4, or are planning to upgrade to CS4 from an earlier version of Photoshop, then this is the obvious choice for you.

If you own neither but know that you will be shooting and processing large numbers of RAW image files, then the choice is more complicated. I recommend Photoshop CS4 for the extra flexibility in the Camera Raw converter and its integration with Bridge, the new File Browser replacement included with CS4, if you're only going to have one program. However, Lightroom 2.1 has so much going for it that it's becoming my main work environment. I still need to go into Photoshop to do some work, but about 80 percent of what I need to do, including all of my RAW conversion work, is now done in Lightroom.

Regardless of which version you choose, or start with, the basic editing options are very similar. Where there are differences between the two versions, I'll call those out for you. If you find that these differences include features that you want or need, then it's time to upgrade to Photoshop CS4.

ADOBE CAMERA Raw Features

	PHOTOSHOP ELEMENTS	PHOTOSHOP CS4 & LIGHTROOM 2.1
16-bit output	Yes	Yes
Save custom settings	No[1]	Yes
White balance tool	Yes	Yes
Preset white balance	Yes	Yes
Temperature adjustment	Yes	Yes
Tint adjustment	Yes	Yes
Exposure adjustment	Yes	Yes
Recovery adjustment	Yes	Yes
Fill light adjustment	Yes	Yes
Blacks adjustment	Yes	Yes
Brightness adjustment	Yes	Yes
Contrast adjustment	Yes	Yes
Clarity adjustment	Yes	Yes
Vibrance adjustment	Yes	Yes
Saturation adjustment	Yes	Yes
Sharpness adjustment	Yes	Yes
Luminance smoothing	Yes	Yes
Color noise reduction	Yes	Yes
Rotate image	Yes	Yes
Resize image	No	Yes
Crop image	Yes	Yes
Straighten image	Yes	Yes
Color samplers	No	Yes
Red-eye removal	Yes	Yes
Shadow/highlight clipping	Yes	Yes
Batch processing	No[2]	Yes
Spot removal	No	Yes
Adjustment brush	No	Yes
Graduated filter	No	Yes
Color spaces	No	Yes
Resolution	No	Yes
Chromatic aberration	No	Yes
Vignetting	No	Yes
Curves	No	Yes
Calibration	No	Yes
HSL/grayscale	No	Yes
Split toning	No	Yes
Presets	No	Yes

1 The Photoshop Elements version of Camera Raw only includes saving settings for Camera Default.

2 Photoshop Elements requires separate steps to apply settings and convert.

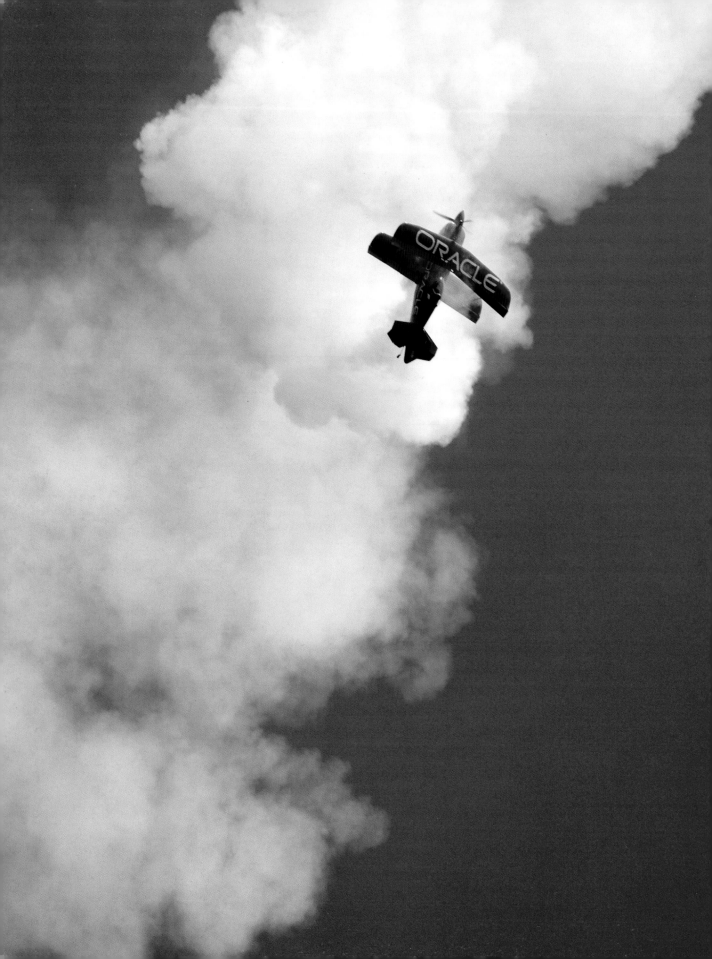

WHAT'S INSIDE

Throughout this book, I'll show you how to get the most detail possible from your RAW files, whether it's correcting shadow and highlight detail, fixing white balance problems, or getting rid of noise. In other words, if you were interested enough in learning about RAW to pick up this book, then you've come to the right place. I've striven to present the topics in a clear and easy-to-understand manner that focuses on results, not technology. Here's what you'll find inside:

> **Chapter 1** presents essential workflow techniques. These are the tasks of getting your images ready for RAW file conversion.

> **Chapter 2** explores the Adobe Camera Raw workspace and Lightroom Develop Module, what the controls are, and how they work on your RAW images.

> **Chapter 3** is all about RAW file conversion and covers the edits that will be done to almost every RAW file you process.

> **Chapter 4** shows you how to go beyond the basics.

> **Chapter 5** covers how to automate Camera Raw to optimize your workflow when converting multiple RAW files.

> **Chapter 6** is all about advanced conversion options for Photoshop CS4 users.

> **Chapter 7** covers the finishing touches you'll commonly have after converting your RAW images.

> **The appendix** provides a complete list of all the keyboard shortcuts available while you're working within Camera Raw.

I love to share information on digital imaging and photography, and I hope this book reflects that passion. I'd love to hear from you with comments about the book, or to share your experiences. I can be contacted at jon@joncanfield.com, or visit my website at www.joncanfield.com. You can also find updates to the information in this book at www.camerarawbook.com.

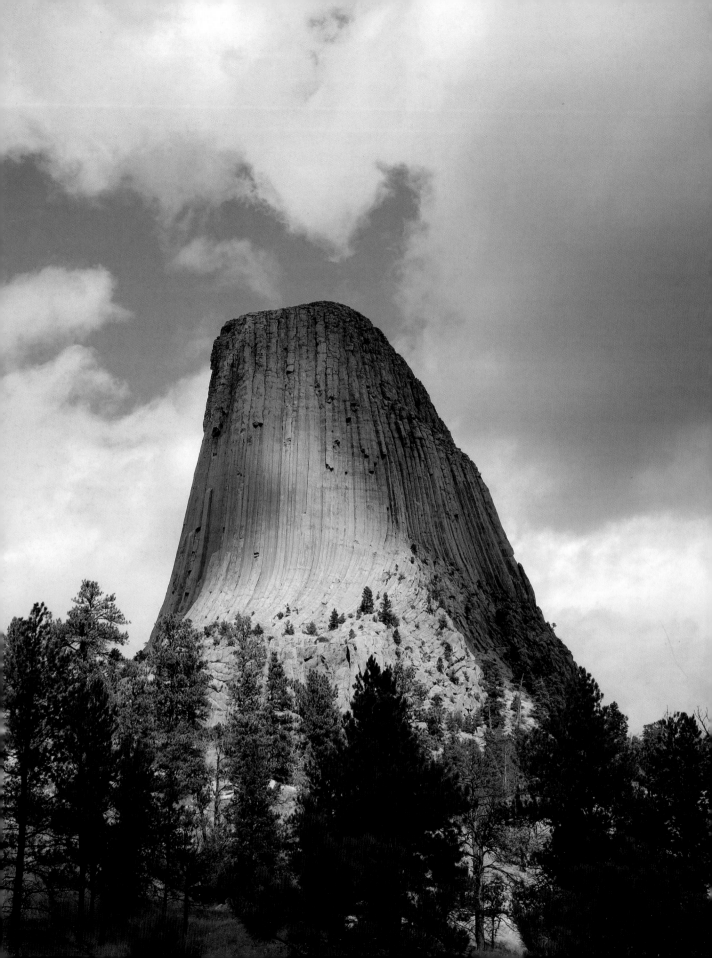

PRELIMINARY WORKFLOW

Shooting digital typically means dealing with large numbers of files. By taking the time to do basic organization tasks and selections, you can reduce the amount of work required to go from shooting session to finished images. In this chapter, I'll cover ways to make managing digital files easier and less time-consuming.

- **Downloading and organizing your images**

- **Using metadata**

- **Rating and flagging images**

- **Selecting images for conversion**

DOWNLOADING AND ORGANIZING YOUR IMAGES

Before you can begin converting your images, you need to get them onto your computer. Mac users can use the Macintosh Image Capture application to handle this, while Windows users with Photoshop Elements have the Organizer and Downloader. Either of these platforms will recognize when a camera or memory card is connected to the computer and will automatically start, making the first step as easy as possible. If you're using Photoshop on either platform, Bridge can be used to copy images and organize them. Because the Macintosh and Windows platforms handle file transfer so differently, I've covered them separately, as I will all platform-specific differences throughout the book in these situations.

Although you can transfer images directly from your camera through a USB or FireWire connection, I prefer to use a card reader for a couple of reasons. First and foremost, transferring directly from your camera means using a power supply or the camera battery. Hooking up a separate power supply is inconvenient, and using battery power means recharging sooner. Regardless of the power source, it also means no more shooting until the transfer is completed. I tend to shoot with multiple memory cards and travel with a laptop for quick edits. Using a card reader allows me to upload images from one card while I continue to shoot using another card.

Which application should you use? If you're using Photoshop Elements on Windows, I recommend using the Downloader application along with Organizer. Macintosh users of Photoshop Elements will be best served by using File Browser. If you're using Photoshop on either platform, I recommend using Bridge to handle your file copies.

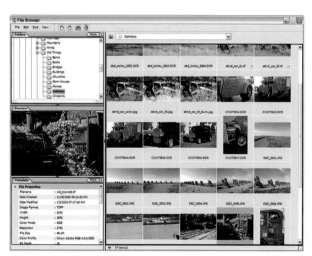 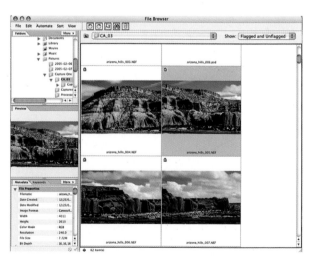

FIGURE 1.1 *Left:* The Windows version of File Browser does not include the Flag or Automate features found in the Macintosh version. *Right:* The Macintosh version looks very similar but includes a Flag files feature and the ability to add keywords.

Using File Browser

Adobe File Browser (**FIGURE 1.1**) is available to both Windows and Macintosh users of Photoshop Elements 6. Photoshop CS4 replaces File Browser with the more powerful Bridge application.

There are some differences between the Mac and Windows versions of File Browser that make a single description of how to use it difficult. The Macintosh version of Photoshop Elements File Browser, perhaps to compensate for not having Adobe Organizer, has been beefed up from previous versions and is now the same as the File Browser included with Photoshop CS.

File Browser is where, on the Macintosh version of Photoshop Elements, you'll add keywords and mark files for editing or deleting. File Browser also contains the search function to help you find the image you are looking for among the hundreds or thousands on your computer.

With both platforms, File Browser can be used to copy images from memory cards to your hard drive. Begin by launching Photoshop Elements and selecting File → Browse Folders.

1. In the Folders panel, select your memory card and the folder that contains your images. In my example from the Macintosh, shown in **FIGURE 1.2**, this would be EOS_DIGITAL:DCIM:100EOS1D.

NOTE: Although iPhoto 5 or later can also be used to copy RAW files, I prefer to use File Browser. This lets me do all of my work in one application.

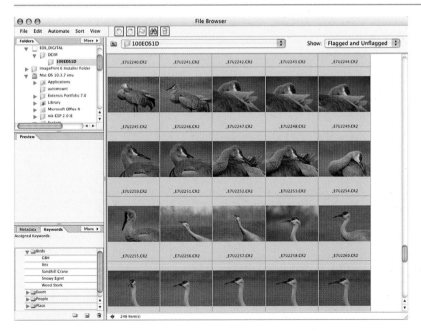

FIGURE 1.2 File Browser can be used to copy images from a memory card to a folder on your computer.

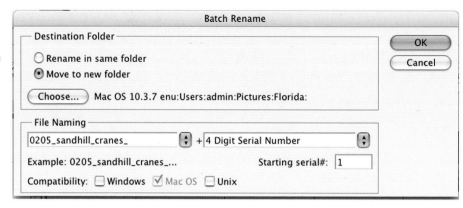

FIGURE 1.3 By using Batch Rename to copy images from a memory card to the computer, you can save a step later in the workflow.

2. After selecting all the images on the card, choose Automate ➔ Batch Rename. Select the "Move to new folder" button and click Choose.

3. Select the folder you want to copy the images to, or create a new one. For my example, I've created a new folder named Florida in my Pictures folder.

4. Give your files a descriptive name (see Renaming Images later in this chapter for suggestions on file naming) and click OK (**FIGURE 1.3**).

NOTE: I've used Batch Rename to copy files for simplicity. Not only does it allow me to create a new folder on the fly, but it also renames the images as they are copied, saving me a step later in the workflow. You could also just drag the files from your memory card to a folder on your computer.

Using Adobe Organizer

Adobe Organizer (**FIGURE 1.4**) is only included with the Windows version of Photoshop Elements. Organizer is essentially a file-cataloging program that makes it easier to sort and find your images.

Organizer makes tagging and finding images simple and relatively painless. Images can be grouped into Collections, which are good ways to organize images of different subjects that are in some way related. As an example, you might create a Summer Vacation collection that contains a variety of images from different sites that don't lend themselves to shared keywords.

Unlike File Browser or Bridge, Organizer only displays images that have been imported, either from a card, camera, or other source. If you have images already on your computer, you can add them to your catalog by selecting File ➔ Get Photos ➔ From Files and Folders (**FIGURE 1.5**).

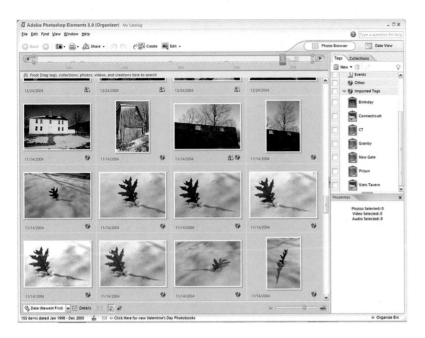

FIGURE 1.4 Organizer is included with the Windows version of Photoshop Elements and is a full-featured image manager.

After selecting the files or folders to import, click the Get Photos button to begin importing images. Organizer will display a progress dialog showing each of the images imported.

Organizer, like most image-management programs, doesn't actually copy the files; it creates a thumbnail of the image. When you select this thumbnail for editing, Organizer goes to the original file and opens it.

When importing into Organizer, only the images just imported will be displayed in the thumbnail window, which makes tagging much easier. Once you've finished tagging or rating images, click the Back to All Photos button to display all images in your catalog.

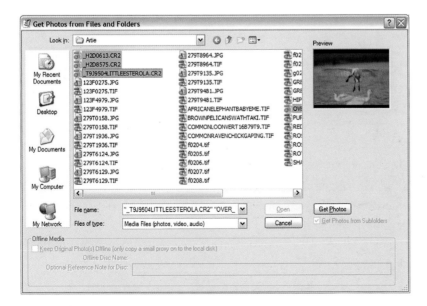

FIGURE 1.5 Importing images already on the computer into Organizer is done with the Get Photos dialog.

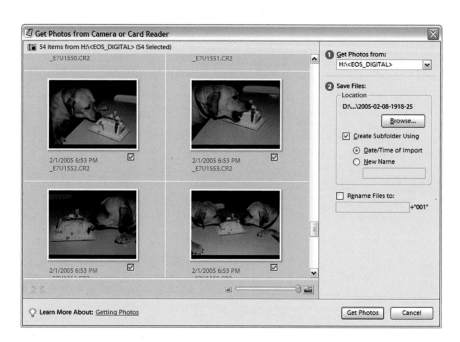

FIGURE I.6 Transferring files on Windows is made easier with the Adobe Downloader.

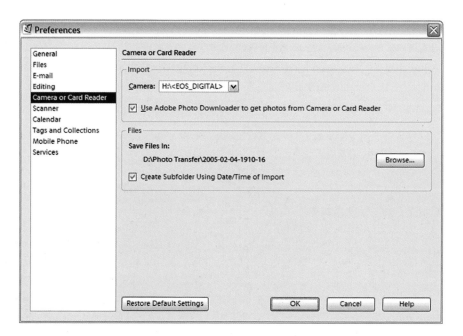

FIGURE I.7 If Downloader isn't starting when your card or camera is connected, check the Preferences setting in Adobe Organizer.

Windows File Transfer with Downloader

Windows users have the same File Browser options as do users of the Macintosh version of Photoshop Elements, but Adobe Organizer, included with the Windows version of Photoshop Elements, adds the very useful Adobe Downloader program (**FIGURE 1.6**) to help get your images out of the camera and onto the computer. Downloader recognizes a device, whether it is a memory card or camera, when plugged into the computer.

To get started with Downloader, connect your camera or insert the memory card into a card reader. Downloader will read and display thumbnails of all the images found on the device, and they can then be selected or excluded from transfer.

If Downloader does not start automatically, open Organizer and select Edit → Preferences → Camera or Card Reader. Make sure the option "Use Adobe Photo Downloader to Get Photos from Camera or Card Reader" is checked, as shown in **FIGURE 1.7**.

When Downloader reads the device, all images will be selected for transfer. Using the checkbox below each thumbnail, you can uncheck any image that you don't want to copy to the computer (**FIGURE 1.8**). This can save some time when there are images that are obviously not worth further review.

NOTE: Most photographers will do at least a quick review in camera and delete inferior images at that time. This not only saves time when transferring images to the computer but also frees up space on the memory card for more shooting.

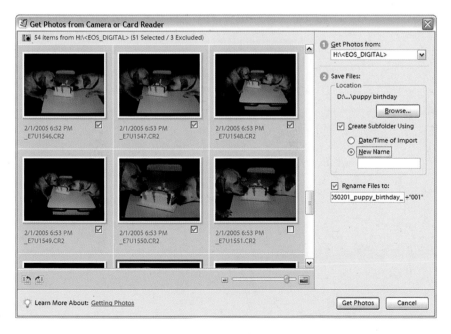

FIGURE 1.8 By default, Downloader will transfer all images on a card. To avoid this, uncheck the box below any image you do not want transferred.

To help make the decision easier, Downloader has a slider to change the size of thumbnails (it's fun to play with, too, if you're as easily amused as I am) located at the lower right side of the preview window. On the lower left side are two buttons to rotate images.

Once you have selected the images to transfer, the next step is to tell Downloader where to place them on your computer. The Save Files area lets you specify where you want the images to be copied and will create a new directory for each transfer. By default, these folders will be created using the date and time of import. You have the option to select the New Name radio button for a custom folder name (**FIGURE 1.9**).

When shooting with multiple subjects, I recommend using the Date/Time of Import setting to keep your images sorted. If all the images being transferred are of the same subject, selecting New Name will allow you to save a step later.

Finally, the Rename Files To option lets you change from the default camera name, typically something like DSC02881, to a more human-friendly name that has some real meaning, like "puppy birthday." File names are appended with a sequential number to keep them unique. I prefer to name by date and subject, so in my example here, files would become 050201_puppy_birthday_001, 050201_puppy_birthday_002, and so on.

NOTE: Using the rename feature means that each directory can have no more than a thousand files using the same starting name. This should be more than sufficient for almost any situation.

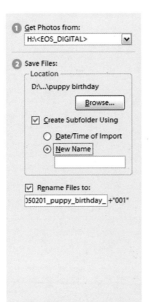

FIGURE 1.9 You can rename the folder Downloader will use when copying images. This can reduce time later when sorting images and make new files easier to find.

Using Adobe Bridge

Bridge works with all of the Adobe CS4 applications and adds the ability to view your images in more detail (**FIGURE 1.10**), rate them for quality, and apply labels to help you find the images you're looking for.

Bridge looks very similar to the File Browser but has several new features that help make this a full-featured image manager, including ratings, labels, the ability to do RAW image processing, and direct access to Photoshop automation tasks such as Web Photo Gallery, Contact Sheets, and Photo Merge.

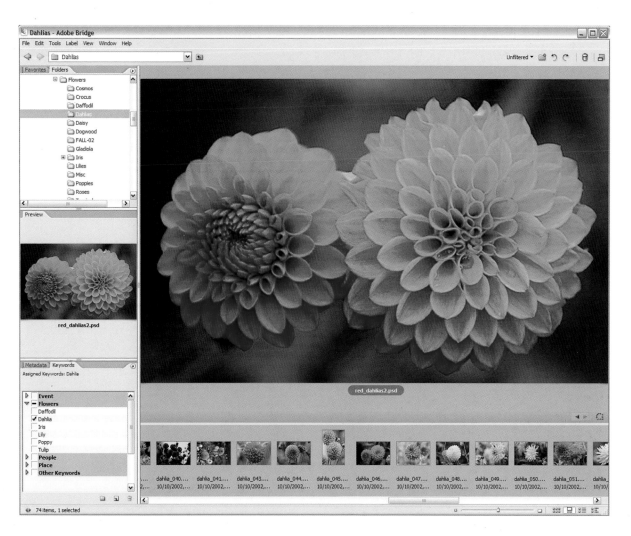

FIGURE 1.10 Bridge is a new feature included with Photoshop CS2 and later versions that replaces File Browser. Image rating and keywords are easy to apply and search on.

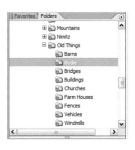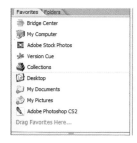

FIGURE 1.11 Folders and Favorites help you find your images quickly in Bridge.

Like File Browser, the Folders, Preview, and Metadata panels are on the left side of the window. Bridge adds a Favorites tab to the Folders panel, making it easier to get to your files (**FIGURE 1.11**) by placing frequently used folders in your Favorites list.

The feature set of Bridge is too large to cover in this book, but if you use Photoshop, it's worth taking a look at Bridge for your image-management needs.

Renaming Images

Establishing a standard naming system will do more to help the initial workflow than almost anything else you can do. As I mentioned earlier when talking about image transfer, the name your camera assigns to an image is less than intuitive. Now imagine browsing through thousands of images with names like _E7U2349.CR2 or DCS22893.NEF and you can easily see the benefit of giving your images more understandable and memorable names.

Luckily, Photoshop Elements and Photoshop both make the renaming process painless. Elements has a Batch Rename function that can be found in File Browser. On Windows, select File ➔ Rename Multiple Files. Macintosh users will select Automate ➔ Batch Rename.

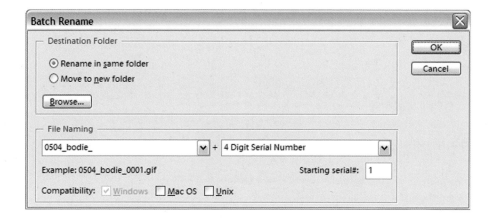

FIGURE 1.12 Using Batch Rename gives a number of options for file naming. I usually use date_ subject_serialnumber.

When renaming images, you have the option to rename the file in the same folder or move the file to a new folder. Unless you have a reason not to, I recommend renaming in the same folder.

Under File Naming there are numerous options available in the list boxes. I normally use the date and subject as the file name with a three- or four-digit serial number. In **FIGURE 1.12**, all the images will be renamed to 0504_bodie_0123.DCR. Bodie is the subject, the images are from May 2004, and 0123 will be the sequential numbers created automatically. Batch rename shows an example of the file name.

Bridge offers more options with Batch Rename, found under Tools → Batch Rename (as shown in **FIGURE 1.13**), including the option to make a copy of the file rather than renaming and moving the original.

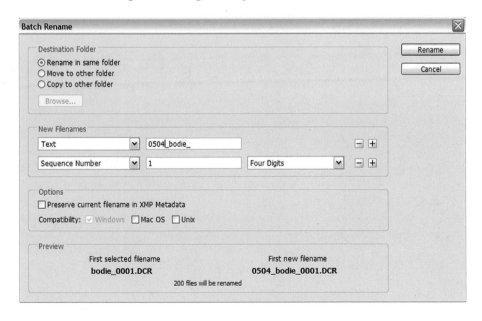

FIGURE 1.13 Batch Rename in Bridge offers more functionality than Photoshop Elements.

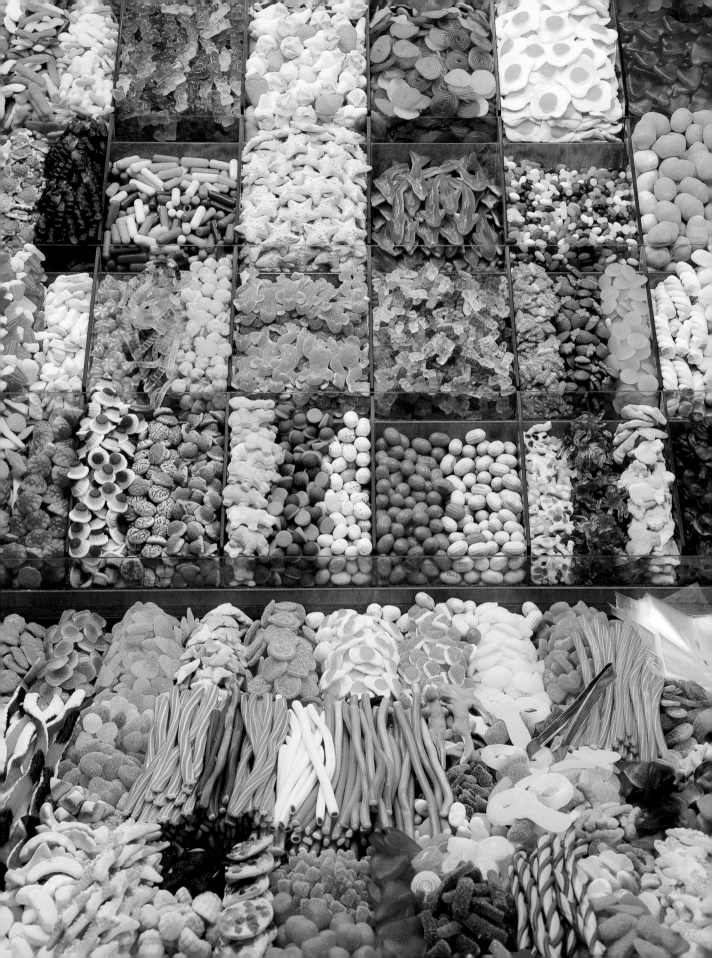

USING METADATA

Metadata is a fancy way of saying "extra information." All digital cameras store metadata, typically in what is known as EXIF format. EXIF, or Exchangeable Image File Format, is a standard way of storing information about the camera and its settings and normally includes date and time, shutter speed, aperture, focal length, flash information, and other shooting data.

In addition to the EXIF data recorded when the photo is taken, most cataloging programs support additional information, or metadata. To help find that image of the heron in a catalog of hundreds or thousands of photos, keywords can be created and assigned to images. Both Photoshop Elements and Photoshop support the addition of metadata to images. In both applications metadata can be created and edited in the File Browser. The Windows version of Elements has an even easier way of assigning metadata by using Organizer's Tags feature.

Defining Keywords

Coming up with a standard naming scheme is a critical part of using metadata. As your image collection grows, you'll appreciate having a list of standard keywords that you can call on to find the photo you are looking for.

I also recommend that you use enough categories and keywords to actually find what you're looking for. Spend some time up front thinking about the kinds of photographs you take and how you usually look for them. A nature photographer is likely to use a completely different set of categories and keywords than a sports photographer, but what the two will have in common is that each subject they shoot can be found by selecting a category and keyword to identify it.

For example, I have tagged some files with the following:

> Mountains (category)
> Cascades
> Eruption
> St. Helens
> Volcano
> Washington

Searching on any of these keywords will find the photo I'm after, but using multiple keywords will narrow down the list significantly. I have mountain images from all over; but if a client calls and needs an image of a volcano in the Cascades, I can select those keywords to search on and reduce the number of images, excluding Mt. Fuji and Mauna Loa from the list, since neither is in the Cascades.

SELECTING IMAGES FOR CONVERSION

Wouldn't it be great if every image we took was perfect and worthy of printing or sharing? It would certainly save time and effort. After all, if all our shots were perfect, we'd probably take fewer photos. And we'd know up front that every photo we took was going to be converted from RAW to TIFF for touchup and other work.

Since every image isn't perfect, many serious photographers tend to have many variations of the same subject. Slight changes to composition, depth of field, and other creative aspects of an image are common and result in a large number of files to review.

Selecting by Keywords

If you've been diligent about assigning keywords, or tags, to your images as you add them to your collection, the easiest way to select images for further processing is by keyword selection.

Bridge and File Browser have very similar search features, as seen in **FIGURES 1.20** and **1.21**.

Multiple keywords can be searched by clicking the + button—up to three with File Browser and up to twelve with Bridge. With File Browser, multiple keywords can only be searched as an AND operation. For example, the search shown in **FIGURE 1.22** will find only images that contain Luke AND Clay as keywords.

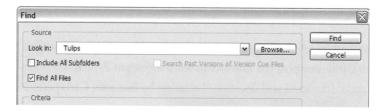

FIGURE 1.20 Bridge Search is accessed by selecting Edit → Find.

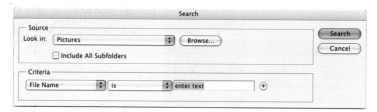

FIGURE 1.21 File Browser Search is accessed by selecting File → Search.

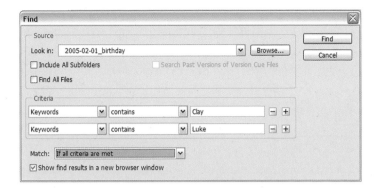

FIGURE I.22 Multiple keywords can be used to narrow down the number of files found.

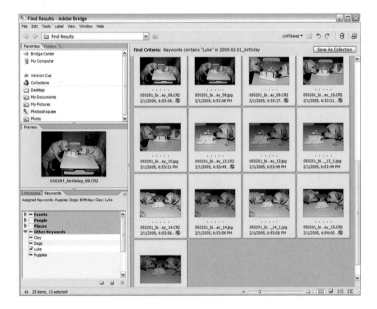

FIGURE I.23 Removing Clay from the search results in the display of all images that have the keyword Luke even if other subjects are in them.

If Clay is removed from the search, then all images that contain Luke will be seen (**FIGURE I.23**).

Bridge has quite a bit more flexibility in its search settings. To match the results in File Browser, click on the Match dropdown list and select "If all criteria are met." To change the search to an OR, select "If any criteria are met." This will find and display any images that have the keywords Luke OR Clay.

The other difference between File Browser and Bridge search dialogs are the criteria you can select from. File Browser has an option to search by flag, while Bridge includes options to search by rating or label.

Organizer handles things a bit differently; its method is one that I have a love-hate relationship with. Rather than using a search dialog, you simply check the boxes next to the tags, or keywords, that you want to find. I love the simplicity of this method. Clicking one or more tags allows you to build a complex selection without much effort. The hate part comes when I am trying to get to the right tags in a group of many.

In the example shown in **FIGURE 1.24**, the tags selected for searching are shown with a binocular icon.

As with File Browser, multiple tag selections work as an AND. In this example, Organizer would find only those images that were tagged with Erin, Kathy, Ken, Bo, Rose, Clay, and Luke. It's not likely that many images would contain all of these tags, so you can modify the search to perform like an OR by clicking the Close checkbox above the thumbnails, as I've done here.

In addition to selecting directly from tags, there is a wealth of options available in the Find menu (**FIGURE 1.25**) that are useful for finding images. In particular, selecting by date range and History come in handy to show only images within a particular set of dates or images that you have submitted or used previously.

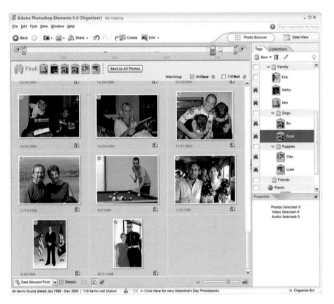

FIGURE 1.24 Searches in Organizer are done by selecting tags.

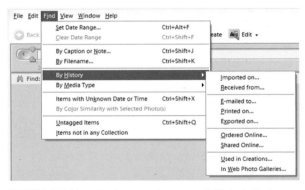

FIGURE 1.25 Additional selection options are available in the Find menu.

FIGURE 1.26 You can build complex searches easily using ratings along with keywords.

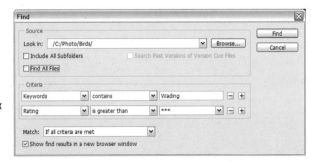

Selecting by Rating and Label

Organizer, Bridge, and iPhoto users can also select by rating. If you have a large group of similar images, it can be effective to make a selection based on keywords and then narrow down the results by using ratings. In Bridge, this can be done as part of the search by adding a rating criterion. **FIGURE I.26** shows a search that will return all of the images with wading birds that are rated four stars or better.

Alternatively, you can narrow down the selection after the search by selecting the rating or label from the Filter list at the top of the Bridge thumbnail view (**FIGURE I.27**).

Rating selections in Organizer are done the same way as other tags. Clicking the box next to the Rating tag will select all images with that rating. To select more than one rating level, click each rating tag you want. For example, selecting the 4 Stars and 3 Stars tags will show all images that are rated at three or four.

In addition to ratings, Bridge adds labels to further help identify images. **FIGURE I.28** shows a Bridge window with rated and labeled thumbnails.

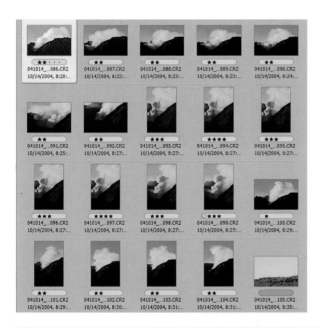

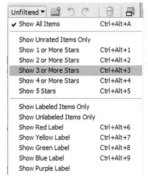

FIGURE I.27 Rating and label selection can also be made from the Filter list in Bridge, or by typing a shortcut.

FIGURE I.28 Bridge also includes labels as a way to further group images.

SUMMARY

I've covered quite a bit of ground in this chapter, and while it may not seem directly about RAW images, establishing a good workflow is critical to the digital darkroom and will make your future image editing more productive, giving you time to work on the images rather than looking for them. Now, let's get on to the good stuff: working with your RAW images!

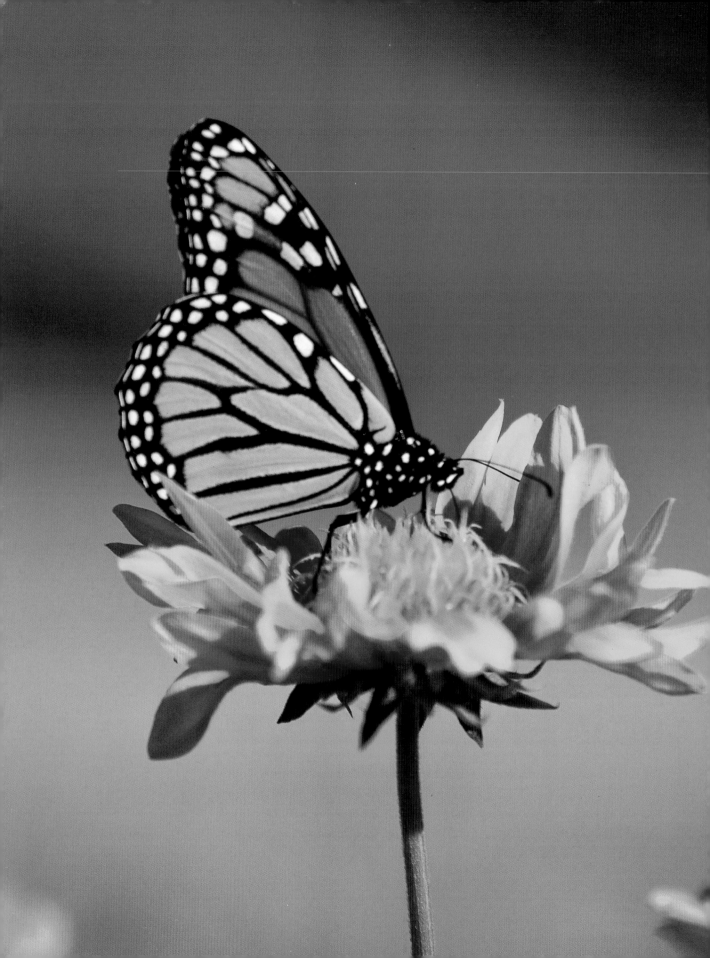

2

ADOBE CAMERA RAW

Photoshop Elements became a legitimate tool for serious photographers with version 3. The ability to work with RAW images and support for 16-bit files means that you can now do most of the editing tasks that previously required Photoshop. In this chapter, I'll introduce you to Adobe Camera Raw (ACR), the conversion tool included in Elements 3. I'll also call out differences between the Photoshop Elements and Photoshop versions of ACR. You'll be happy to know that for the majority of users, ACR and Elements can handle all the RAW processing tasks you might have.

- **Camera Raw versus other converters**

- **Using the preview area**

- **Setting bit depth**

- **Shadows and highlights clipping**

- **Understanding the histogram**

- **Understanding the adjustment sliders and Auto option**

- **Fine-tuning**

CAMERA RAW VERSUS OTHER CONVERTERS

With so many options available for RAW image conversion, why should you consider Adobe Camera Raw? After all, your camera most likely came with conversion software that may be as basic as Nikon View, which offers basic correction to white balance and exposure, or as full featured as Canon's Digital Photo Pro, which gives you full access to everything that you might want to do with a RAW file prior to conversion.

NOTE: I don't include the very capable Nikon Capture in this list because it is a separate purchase—an error on Nikon's part, in my mind.

In my experience, camera companies are much better at designing cameras than they are at designing software, and when you use most of these tools, it shows. "Good user interface" and "performance" are not terms usually associated with the provided conversion tools.

There are also numerous other tools available to handle the processing tasks, and some of them are quite good indeed, rivaling Adobe Camera Raw for functionality and quality. In particular, Capture One from Phase One (www.phaseone.com) and Lightzone from Lightcrafts (www.lightcrafts.com) are both very powerful converters that operate on both Macintosh and Windows systems and provide the user with a wealth of RAW conversion options.

The one thing that none of these options provides is a tight integration with Photoshop or Photoshop Elements. Adobe has invested considerable time and effort into making ACR one of the premier converters available, and it shows. The advantages to ACR are apparent from the start if you are a Photoshop (**FIGURE 2.1**) or Elements user (**FIGURE 2.2**). The dialog and controls are laid out in a consistent and familiar way to keep the learning curve to a minimum.

Camera Raw also has another advantage that shouldn't be overlooked or underestimated: If you change camera brands at some point (and many of us do), there are no new programs to learn. If ACR supports the RAW files produced by your camera, it will look and work the same, regardless of camera type. As someone who has gone from one manufacturer to another, this converter "sameness" is both comforting and productive; I spend time perfecting images rather than learning software.

Finally, if you're just starting out with image editing and have chosen Photoshop Elements, or you work in an environment with both Elements and Photoshop, it's nice to know that if you move up to Photoshop the RAW converter you've learned is still there with the same interface and controls along with a handful of new and useful advanced tools.

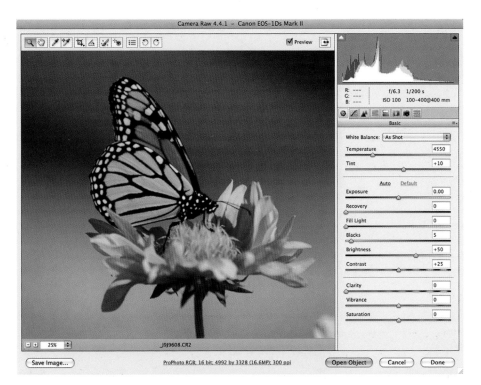

FIGURE 2.1 The version of Adobe Camera Raw included with Photoshop CS4 offers more options than the Elements version, but both use the same conversion process.

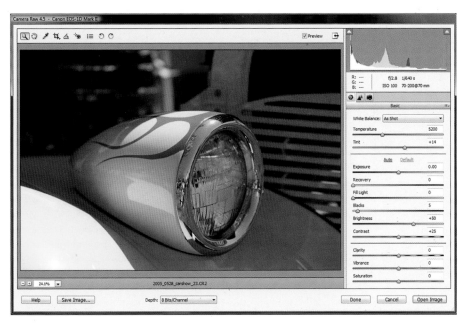

FIGURE 2.2 Befitting the easier, "less is more approach" that Elements takes, the version of ACR included here has fewer options (note the lack of tabs) but the same general layout.

USING THE PREVIEW AREA

The preview area of ACR is used for overall previews (kind of makes sense, doesn't it?) of all editing operations you'll be performing on the RAW image prior to conversion. Since Photoshop Elements and Photoshop have different tools, I'll cover each separately. **FIGURE 2.3** shows the preview area along with the controls available to help with image correction.

In contrast, there are fewer controls available in the Photoshop Elements version of Camera Raw, as seen in **FIGURE 2.4**. This version of Camera Raw is essentially the same as the one included with the earlier release of Photoshop CS but adds Auto settings.

Above the Preview window, you'll find a toolbar of icons for basic tasks. **FIGURE 2.5**. shows the two different toolbars you'll see depending on which version of Camera Raw you're using.

FIGURE 2.3 The preview area of Photoshop CS4's version of Camera Raw will help you determine the best options for the image prior to conversion and lets you crop and straighten an image.

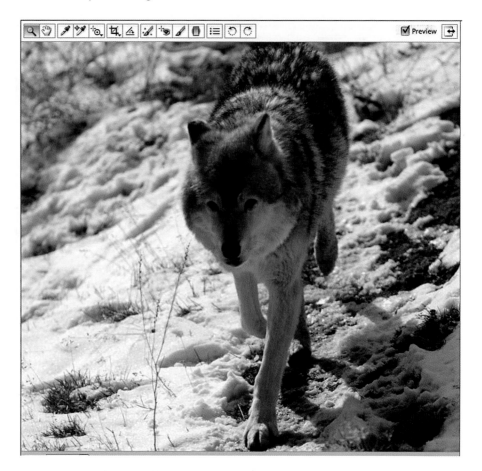

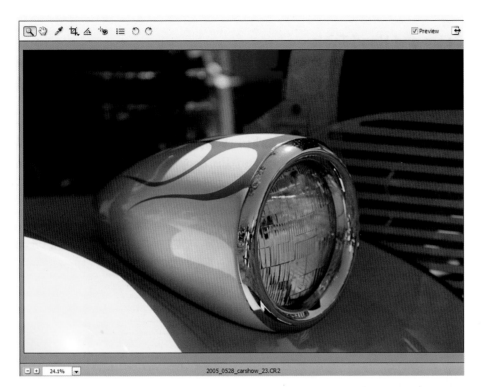

FIGURE 2.4 The preview area for Photoshop Elements Camera Raw is laid out a bit differently and has fewer options available than does that of Photoshop CS4.

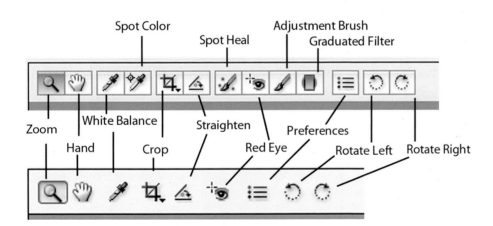

FIGURE 2.5 The toolbar in Camera Raw contains several basic image-editing tools. The toolbar in CS4, shown on top, has a few more tools than does the Elements version, bottom.

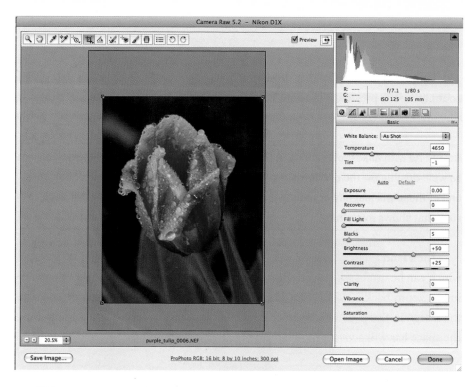

FIGURE 2.9 The selected area will be converted and opened in Photoshop at the size selected. In this example, the image will be 8 x 10 at 300 dpi.

When you crop in Camera Raw, as seen in **FIGURE 2.9**, the converted the image will be opened at the selected size in Photoshop.

The Straighten tool is in reality a crop tool with a helpful line to straighten horizons. To use the Straighten tool, select it in the toolbar. Next, click at the starting point and drag across to the ending point, as shown in **FIGURE 2.10**. When you release the mouse button, a crop will be created with the angle you selected.

NOTE: You can straighten a horizon with the Crop tool as well. Just move the mouse pointer to the masked area of the image, and it will change to a curved double arrow. Dragging up or down will rotate the crop selection.

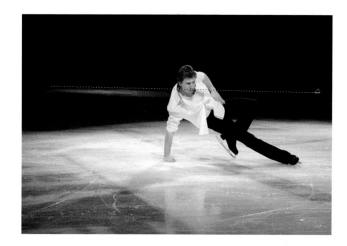
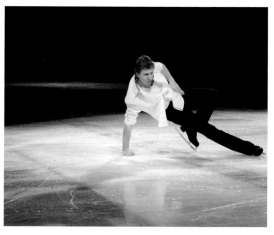

FIGURE 2.10 The Straighten tool can help you quickly and accurately correct a horizon that is "level challenged."

Rotate Tools

Rotate Image 90 degrees counterclockwise ↺ and Rotate Image 90 degrees clockwise ↻ tools let you do a nondestructive quarter turn of your image prior to conversion. Rotate is pretty obvious: Clicking simply turns the image 90 degrees in the indicated direction. The Rotate tools also work by typing R or L on the keyboard.

White Balance Tool

The White Balance tool ✎ can help you quickly correct color balance problems in a RAW image. The tool works by sampling the color under the pointer. When that color is selected by clicking the mouse button, it becomes neutral in tone. To help determine whether a color is close to neutral in tone, the R, G, and B (**FIGURE 2.11**) values are updated as the pointer is moved.

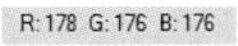

R: 178 G: 176 B: 176

FIGURE 2.11 As you move the mouse pointer around the image area, the R: G: B: values will change, showing you the relative amount of each color in that area of the image. Clicking the mouse with the White Balance tool will set all three color values to equal.

NOTE: Regardless of the tool you have selected, holding down the Alt/Option key will activate the Zoom Out tool, and the Shift key will activate the White Balance tool. Releasing the key will return you to your regularly scheduled tool.

ACR offers multiple ways to select a color balance for your image. The most obvious of these are the White Balance dropdown list, shown in **FIGURE 2.12**, *top*, and the Temperature slider, shown in **FIGURE 2.12**, *bottom*. The dropdown list is a great way to set gross white balance adjustments. By gross, I mean major changes, such as when the image was captured with a Daylight white balance but the camera should have been set to Tungsten.

The Temperature slider can be used to move to a particular color temperature using the Kelvin scale. Kelvin uses a very wide range of temperatures, with midday sunlight typically around 5,500. **TABLE 2.1** provides a more complete list of average temperatures.

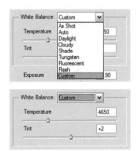

FIGURE 2.12 The White Balance dropdown list (*top*) has defaults for most normal lighting conditions. This can be a useful first step in getting the color correct in your images. The Temperature slider (*bottom*) can then be used to fine-tune the color.

TABLE 2.1: Approximate Kelvin Values for Common Lighting

TYPE OF LIGHTING	TYPICAL TEMPERATURE
Candlelight	1,900
Sunrise/sunset	2,000
Incandescent (tungsten)	2,800–3,200
Fluorescent (warm)	3,000
Halogen	3,000
Photofloods	3,200
Fluorescent (cool white)	3,800
Sunlight (morning/evening)	4,300
Sunlight (midday)/flash	5,500
Cloudy	6,500
Shade	7,500
Blue sky	12,000+

One technique that I find useful is to select a preset white balance from the list, such as Daylight, and then adjust the Temperature slider to give the image a look that is a bit warmer or cooler.

For those times when you need absolute control over the white balance, or when you want to set a neutral point for your image but not remove a desired color cast, the White Balance tool can make the job a little easier. By clicking on an area that should be neutral in tone, you can eliminate any colorcast that might be in the image. Neutral doesn't mean 18% gray, which is the standard neutral gray for which a camera's meter is calibrated; rather, it means any tone that is equal parts red, green, and blue. So, clicking on an area in your image with the White Balance tool will cause that to become the neutral balance that all colors are adjusted to. In **FIGURE 2.13**, I've clicked on the clouds, since they should be equal parts of all three color channels.

FIGURE 2.13 Clicking on a pixel in your image with the White Balance tool will cause that color to become neutral in value with all color channels containing the same value and all other colors adjusting accordingly.

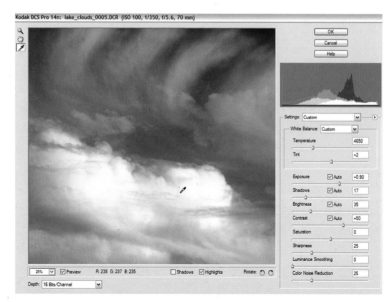

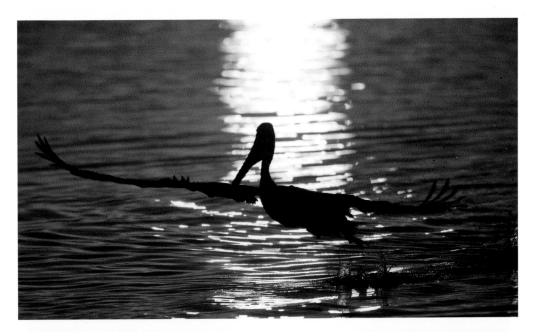

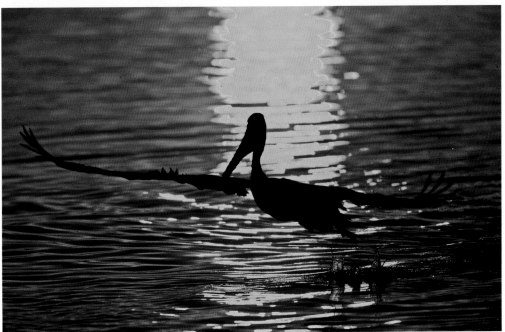

FIGURE 2.14 *Top*: This image was adjusted for color temperature to be neutral in tone. While it's a very nice image, it has none of the warmth and atmosphere of the original image. *Bottom*: Same image, but with the correct color temperature. The rich golden light adds to the impact of the image. (Courtesy Art Morris, www.birdsasart.com)

Why would you want to leave a colorcast in the image? Ask any nature photographer and you'll probably get the same answer: golden light at morning or evening. There are times when we strive for a particular feel to our images; the bottom image in **FIGURE 2.14** is an example of this golden light. Without it, the image is a technically nice image but lacks the feeling of the original scene.

The Tint slider, located just below the Temperature slider, can be further used to control the tint of your image, warming or cooling as desired. The Tint slider is most effectively used in combination with the White Balance tool. By adjusting the Tint slider to the left, or negative numbers, you add more green to the image. Positive numbers to the right add more red.

NOTE: You can use the keyboard to adjust temperature and tint. The up and down arrows will adjust temperature by 50 and tint by I. Adding Shift adjusts by 500 and I0 respectively.

Color Sampler Tool (Photoshop CS4 Only)

The Color Sampler tool ✎ lets you take up to four measurements. The only real value I can see in the Color Sampler is when you are using the Calibrate options. I'll cover this in Chapter 6, Advanced Conversion Options.

Workflow Settings

The final area of the Preview window to look at is the Workflow Settings. As with the Toolbar options, Photoshop has more options here as well (**FIGURE 2.15**) than the version of Camera Raw included with Elements.

Photoshop has full color-management support and lets you select from four different color spaces when converting a RAW file. Of the four, Adobe RGB (1998) is the most commonly used color space and an appropriate choice for general image editing. ProPhoto RGB has a bit larger color space than Adobe RGB (1998) and is preferred by many pro shooters for the slightly wider color range possible. sRGB IEC61966-1 is designed for screen display, such as Web browsers or digital slide-shows. Unless you know in advance that your image conversion is going to be used only for screen display, Adobe RGB (1998) or ProPhoto RGB will be the best choices.

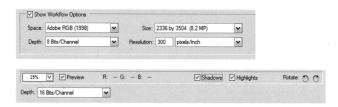

FIGURE 2.15 *Top*: The Photoshop CS4 Workflow Settings contains options for setting the bit depth, color space, resolution, and image size. *Bottom*: The Elements version of Camera Raw has fewer options than its big brother. You'll be able to set the bit depth, preview size, and rotation, as well as highlight and shadow warnings.

SETTING BIT DEPTH

The Depth setting offers two choices: 8 Bits/Channel and 16 Bits/Channel. 8-bit images contain a maximum of 256 values per color; 16-bit images, on the other hand, provide 32,768 possible values per color. This extra bit depth is one of the reasons to shoot RAW over JPEG. When saving a file at 8 Bits/Channel, color information is discarded, reducing both image quality and the ability to make editing changes without significant image degradation. Since you shoot RAW for maximum image quality, I recommend using the 16 Bits/Channel setting to retain all the color information in your original file.

NOTE: If you know that a file will be used only on the Web or in a slideshow, 8 Bits/Channel might seem like a logical choice. I recommend always converting at 16 Bits/Channel and doing all image edits before converting to 8 Bits/Channel as the final step.

Many of the editing tasks that you'll be doing after conversion from RAW to TIFF are considered destructive edits—i.e., image data is changed and cannot be recovered. When working with 8 bits of data per color, these changes are seen much more quickly, leading to loss of image quality with fairly minor adjustments (see **FIGURE 2.16**). By working in 16 bits, you have much more latitude in your adjustments, able to make larger changes without a visible loss of detail.

Bit depth is the one case in which I would suggest that you always use the highest setting or level possible. If you are going to take the time and effort to shoot in RAW for maximum quality, why immediately throw out color information before you even get started?

Of course, high-bit-depth files have their unique drawbacks. Chief among these is file size. A 16-bit TIFF file is going to be roughly twice the size of its 8-bit counterpart. Consider a typical RAW file from the Canon 1D Mark II. As a RAW file, it uses about 8MB of disk space. Opening that file as an 8-bit TIFF increases the size to 23.4MB. That same file converted to a 16-bit TIFF uses 46.8MB of disk space.

FIGURE 2.16 One of the biggest advantages to shooting in RAW is the additional bit depth available in your image. RAW captures are typically 10 to 14 bits per color channel. The color bar on the left is 8-bit color, while the one on the right uses 14-bit color and has smoother transitions.

SHADOWS AND HIGHLIGHTS CLIPPING

Here's some advice: Make life easier for yourself and turn on Shadows and Highlights clipping by clicking on the indicators in the upper left and right corners of the histogram. This is far and away the best tool, in combination with the histogram, in Adobe Camera Raw to monitor exposure information in your images. Without these two options enabled, you're just guessing at how much detail you can pull from your photo.

As an example, I'll start with the image shown in **FIGURE 2.17**. I know that this image has room for improvement in the shadows and highlights because the histogram shows the image data ending before it reaches either end of the histogram.

To start with, I'll add more detail in the shadows through the Shadows slider. To increase shadow detail, I move the slider to the right. As soon as I pass the maximum for the image, the preview shows information that is beyond the useable range in bright blue (**FIGURE 2.18**). At this point, back off the shadow level until the blue is gone.

Repeating the process for the highlights, I adjust the Exposure slider until I see bright red (**FIGURE 2.19**). Again, I back off the exposure level until the red is gone.

Not every image needs to have the maximum shadow and highlight detail. There are some images, such as high key or low key, that would not benefit from both of these adjustments. I'll cover these types of images later, but for now it's good to know how to verify that your image isn't going beyond the limits of what you can display or print.

FIGURE 2.17 This image needs more shadow detail. By turning on the Shadows clipping warning, I can see when I've gone as far as possible.

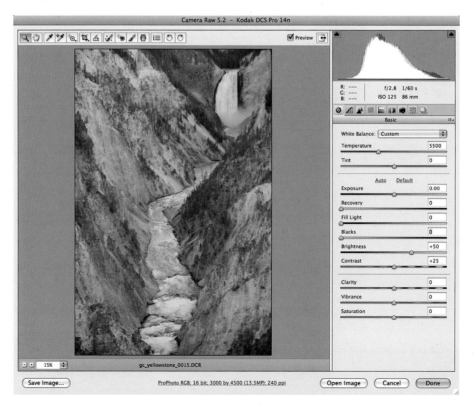

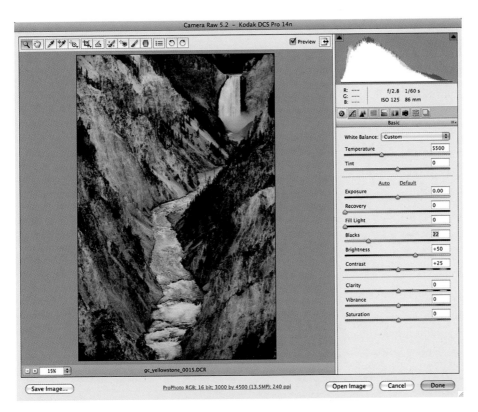

FIGURE 2.18 The bright blue spots (at bottom right and along the riverbank) indicate areas that have lost all detail and will display as pure black.

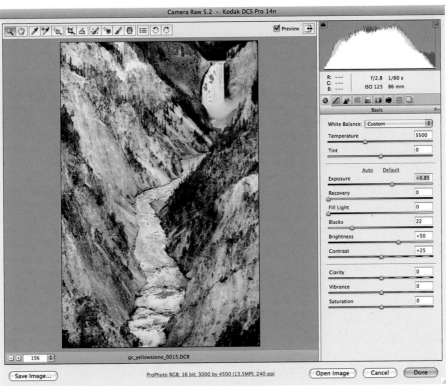

FIGURE 2.19 Clipped highlights are displayed in bright red when the Highlights checkbox in the upper right area of the histogram is selected.

UNDERSTANDING THE HISTOGRAM

The histogram is your key to understanding where color values are in the image. A histogram represents the range of tone from pure black on the left to pure white on the right. The height of the columns in the histogram indicates how much of the data of that tone are present in the image. For example, in the histogram shown in **FIGURE 2.20**, there are very few pixels in the image that are black or white, but the bulk of the pixels are in the upper mid-tones, which are represented by the taller bars in the histogram.

Ideally, your images will have all the data between these two end points, whether the data are distributed evenly from dark to light, or exposed as far to the right as possible without losing, or clipping, highlight information. The image shown in **FIGURE 2.20** is an example of a well-exposed photo. All of the image data lay between the black and white end points of the histogram.

If you view your image and see a histogram similar to the ones in **FIGURE 2.21**, you know that either the exposure was wrong or the dynamic range of the image was wider than the camera was able to capture. Image information that is beyond the range the camera can capture will be displayed as pure black or pure white.

FIGURE 2.20 This image is properly exposed. All image data are contained within the histogram, which shows that no information is being lost, or "clipped," at either end of the scale.

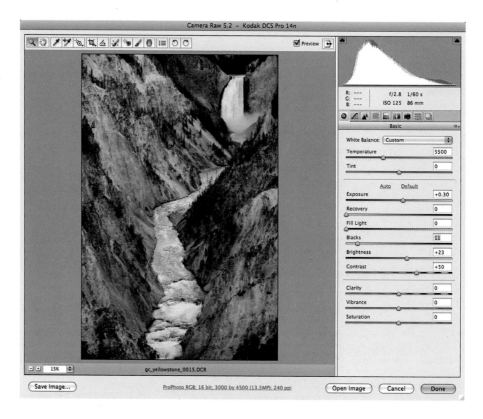

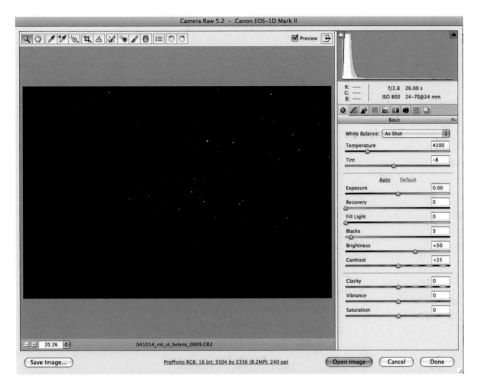

FIGURE 2.21 *Top*: This histogram is from an image that is underexposed. Most of the data in this image are in the left side of the histogram. Every pixel at the left edge of the histogram will be displayed as pure black. *Bottom*: The histogram for an overexposed image.

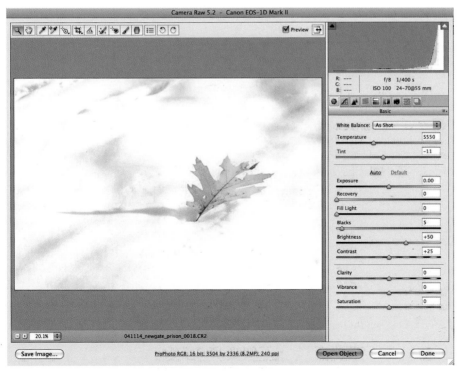

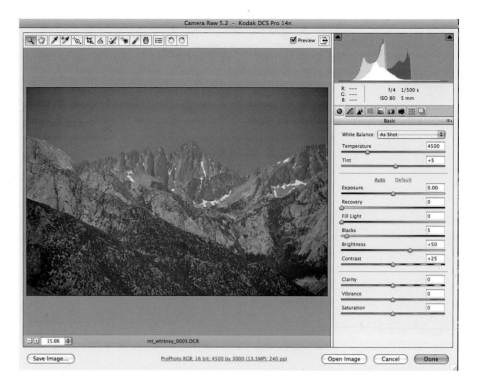

FIGURE 2.22 When all the image information is bunched together in the histogram, the image will look flat with no true shadow or highlight detail. This is easy to correct with the adjustment sliders.

Another area of potential problem for your image is when all the data in the histogram are bunched together with empty space between the edges of the histogram and the start of your image information, as shown in **FIGURE 2.22**. This type of histogram indicates a flat image that is lacking true shadows and highlights. Luckily, this is also the easiest one to correct-all the image information is there and usable; it's up to you to bring that detail out through adjustments to exposure, shadows, highlights, and contrast.

The histogram is one of the most valuable tools at your disposal when making adjustments to the image. By monitoring the effect of changes to exposure, shadows, highlights, and contrast, you can maximize the tonal range of your image while preventing detail from being lost through adjustments that are too aggressive. In the next section, I'll show you how to use both the histogram and the Shadows and Highlights warnings to get the most from your RAW file prior to conversion.

The histogram displays red, green, and blue values individually. In addition to these colors, cyan, magenta, yellow, and white will also be displayed in the histogram (**FIGURE 2.23**). These colors show where there is overlap between the different color channels:

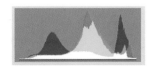

FIGURE 2.23 The histogram display shows each color channel and the number of pixels that contain data for multiple color channels.

> **Cyan** indicates pixels in which both blue and green are present.
> **Magenta** represents the overlap between red and blue.
> **Yellow** shows pixels that contain both red and green.
> **White** indicates pixels that have data from all three color channels.

UNDERSTANDING THE ADJUSTMENT SLIDERS AND AUTO OPTION

All versions of Camera Raw have a feature that has the promise of saving you time with image adjustments. I say "promise" because it isn't a cure-all. The Exposure, Shadows, Highlights, and Contrast sliders all have an Auto checkbox, as shown in **FIGURE 2.24**. Auto for these controls works similarly to the Auto Levels, Contrast, and Color settings you may be used to from the Image → Adjustments menu in Photoshop CS and the Enhance menu in Photoshop Elements.

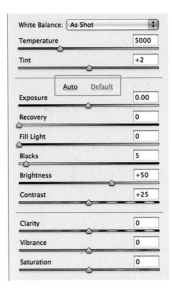

FIGURE 2.24 Adobe Camera Raw now includes an Auto option for common image correction. Like the Auto Levels, Contrast, and Color settings from Photoshop and Photoshop Elements, they aren't the perfect choice for every image but can serve as a good starting point for your corrections.

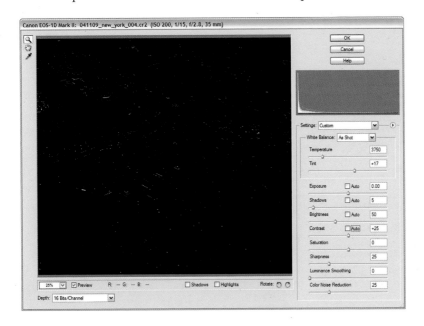

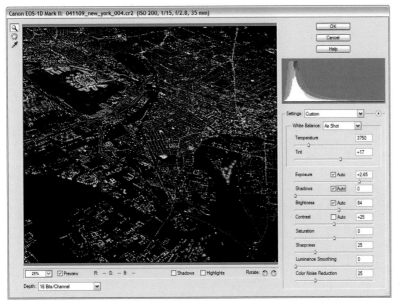

FIGURE 2.25 *Top*: New York from the air. With Auto settings disabled, the image is primarily black with a few dots of light. *Bottom*: The same image with Auto checked for each of the controls shows the detail and scene as I remember it.

Like any Auto feature, it's important to understand how the setting works and when it should or shouldn't be used. Chapter 3 goes into detail on using each of these controls to fine-tune your image. The examples here show how the Auto settings can work for you . . . and against you.

The Auto settings can be a useful starting point for your image corrections though. **FIGURE 2.25** shows an admittedly extreme example of what the Auto checkboxes can do for you. This shot of the New York area from an airplane goes from almost black to a well-exposed image with only the Auto settings.

FIGURE 2.26 *Top*: This image is going to lose significant amounts of shadow and highlight detail if the Auto settings are used. *Bottom*: By setting these controls manually, I am able to retain detail that would have been otherwise lost.

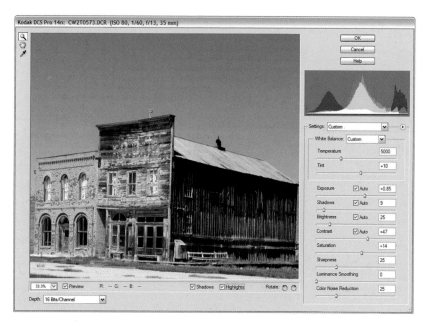

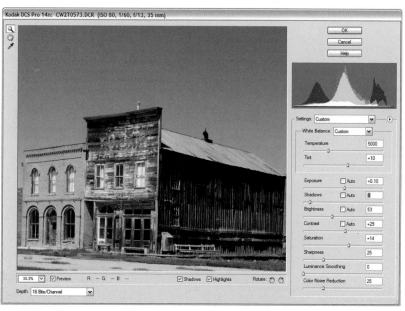

In contrast to the New York photo, the image from Bodie shown in **FIGURE 2.26** (*top*) is an example of what happens when the Auto settings are too aggressive. With the Highlights and Shadows checkboxes enabled, it's clear that the Auto settings added too much exposure and shadow to the image, resulting in lost data. Making these adjustments manually, I was able to retain significant detail that would have been lost at both ends of the tonal range (as shown in the bottom image).

NOTE: You can't hurt the image at this point by playing with the adjustment settings. Try the Auto settings on your image to see if they work. It may be that you only need a slight adjustment.

Exposure

The Exposure slider allows you to make adjustments of up to four stops over or under to your RAW image. Using the Exposure slider is similar to setting exposure compensation in the camera when you capture the image. Unlike compensation set in camera, though, modifying the exposure in Camera Raw will not recover information that is not there. In other words, if you've over—or underexposed the image to the point of no information other than black or white being recorded, the Exposure slider isn't going to magically get that data back for you. Adjustments to the Exposure slider can help make shadow areas less dense and highlights less bright, which will allow subtle detail that was hiding in those areas to be more obvious.

The Auto setting for exposure works very similarly to the Auto Levels command in Photoshop and Photoshop Elements. It works by analyzing the image data and making adjustments to maximize the amount of tonal range in your image.

NOTE: Maximizing the tonal range is normally a good thing but is not appropriate for all images. High-key images, for example, would have the majority of their tonal range at the highlight side of the histogram. Spreading this out across the entire possible range would take away from the effect.

The Exposure slider determines the brightness of the entire image, setting the brightest value the image will contain. If you are familiar with the Levels control, Exposure works like the right slider in the Levels dialog (**FIGURE 2.27**).

The most effective way to use the Exposure control is by using the Shadows and Highlights clipping checkboxes and the Alt/Option key method.

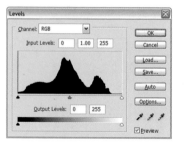

FIGURE 2.27 The Exposure, Blacks, and Brightness sliders work like the controls in Photoshop and Photoshop Elements Levels control. Exposure controls the right slider, Blacks the left slider, and Brightness the center slider.

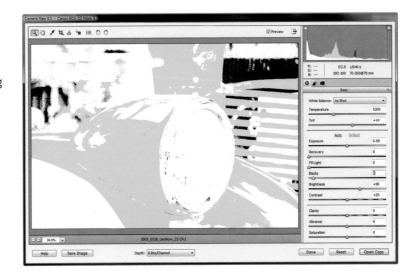

FIGURE 2.28 By holding down the Alt/Option key while adjusting the Blacks slider, you can easily see when detail is beginning to "clip," or go out of range.

Blacks

The Blacks slider controls the black point in your image. Blacks is equivalent to the black point or left slider in the Levels command. The Blacks slider has a range of 0 to 100, but typically you'll use values of 25 or less. The default setting for Blacks is 2 when Auto is unchecked. As with Exposure, the best way to monitor adjustments with the Blacks slider is by using the Alt/Option key while making adjustments (**FIGURE 2.28**).

Brightness

The Brightness slider works to set the overall brightness of your image without affecting the shadow or highlights. Like the Exposure and Shadows sliders, it also has an equivalent in the Levels command. Brightness works in the same manner as the center slider. To brighten the overall tone of the image, move the slider to the right. The slider has a range of 0 to 150 and defaults to 50 when Auto is unchecked.

When using the Brightness slider, you'll need to keep an eye on the histogram to see where the color values are going to ensure that you don't begin clipping colors.

Contrast

The Contrast slider can add depth to your image and really make it come to life. With a range of –50 to 100, the default setting is 25 when Auto is unchecked. Settings higher than 25 will add more contrast by darkening the values below the mid-tone and lightening those above it. Reducing the setting below 25 will reduce contrast in the image by lightening the values below the mid-tone and darkening the values above it.

FINE-TUNING

The final four controls that are in common with both Photoshop Elements and Photoshop CS4 versions of Camera Raw are Saturation, Sharpness, Luminance Smoothing, and Color Noise Reduction. Photoshop Elements users will find all four of these sliders displayed below Contrast. Photoshop CS4 users will see the Saturation slider on this tab while the others are found on the Detail tab (**FIGURE 2.29**).

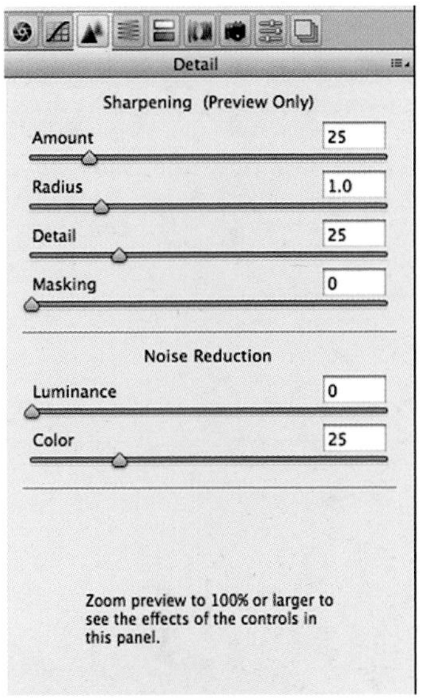

Saturation

Saturation defaults to 0 and is often best left there. Possible values range from –100 to 100. This is one of the few options that I prefer to wait until post-processing to do. Since the amount of saturation needed will change depending on the intended use of the image, I feel that it is best done after conversion.

NOTE: You can make a quick conversion to grayscale by setting the Saturation slider to –100. You won't have the same level of control that you would by using the Channel Mixer, but it is possible to create a good black-and-white image during conversion by this method. After setting Saturation to the far left, adjustments to contrast, exposure, shadows, and brightness can yield good results that would otherwise take several steps in Photoshop CS4 or Photoshop Elements. I'll cover this technique in depth in chapter 4. Even better, if you're using CS4 or Lightroom, you can use the HSL controls, which are covered in chapter 6.

FIGURE 2.29 The Detail tab in the Photoshop CS4 version of Camera Raw contains the Sharpness, Luminance Smoothing, and Color Noise Reduction sliders.

Sharpness

Every digital image needs sharpening. That may sound like a bold statement, but it's true, especially for cameras that use an anti-aliasing filter (which most do) to reduce moiré, which is the appearance of wavy colored lines, or sometimes a maze type of pattern, in the photo. Camera Raw includes a Sharpness slider, so it would seem logical to use this to sharpen your image, right? Wrong! The problem with sharpening in Camera Raw is that you have very little control over how the sharpening is applied. It's also best to apply sharpening as one of the last steps in image processing, since you'll have different needs depending on your output size and type. The sharpening you apply to a Web image will almost certainly not be the same as what you would apply to the same image for printing.

The Sharpness slider is a handy tool, though, for use while previewing your RAW adjustments. In Photoshop CS4 and Elements 6 or 7, to make sure that only the preview is sharpened and not the converted file, you can set the default in Camera Raw Preferences to Preview Image Only. Click on the triangle next to the Settings list and select Preferences. In the Camera Raw Preferences dialog, select Preview Images Only from the Apply Sharpening To list. This is not an option with Lightroom, though, since sharpening is done only when the file is exported.

Luminance Smoothing

Luminance Smoothing controls the noise in the image that appears similar to film grain. This type of noise is usually apparent in digital images with dense shadow areas and those shot at higher ISO settings. Any adjustment to reduce this type of noise will soften the image, so it's best to critically examine the image during adjustment. I suggest zooming in to at least 100 percent on the area that you are concerned about and using the keyboard to make adjustments to Luminance Smoothing. The up and down arrow keys will make a one-step change with each key press.

Color Noise Reduction

Unlike the noise controlled with the Luminance Smoothing slider, Color Noise Reduction works on those irritating green- and magenta-toned spots that show up predominantly in the shadow areas of your images, like in the one shown in **FIGURE 2.30**.

As with the Luminance Smoothing slider, it's critical to make minor adjustments while viewing the image at 100 percent or larger. Color Noise Reduction will also soften the image. It's up to you to decide whether the softness is objectionable.

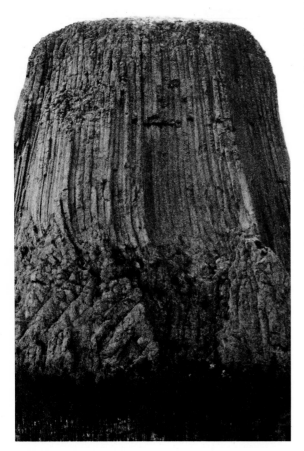

FIGURE 2.30 Color noise is typically seen as green and magenta spots in the shadow areas of your image. It's more likely to occur with high ISO or long exposures.

Other Camera Raw Controls

Photoshop CS4 and Lightroom users will find additional controls in Camera Raw available to adjust chromatic aberration, lens vignetting, curves adjustment, and camera calibration. I'll cover all of these controls in chapter 6, Advanced Conversion Options.

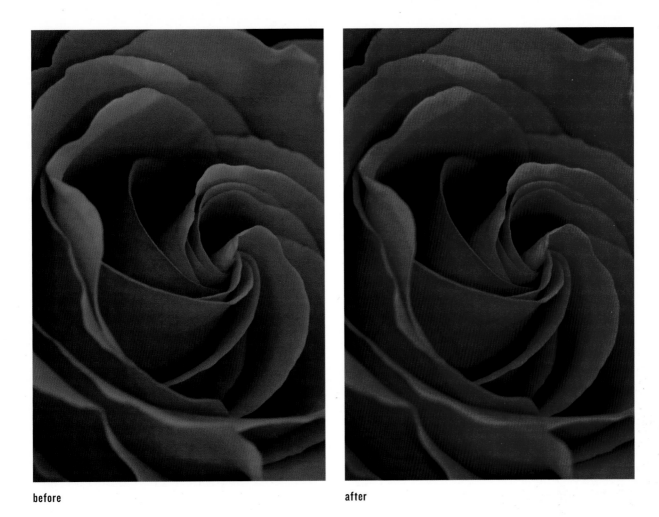

before   **after**

FIGURE 2.31 The before image of this rose is straight from the camera, no adjustments, while the after version has been converted for color balance, exposure, and blacks.

SUMMARY

Adobe Camera Raw has many options to help you convert your RAW images. Whether you use the version of Camera Raw in Photoshop Elements 6 or 7 or the more advanced version included with Photoshop CS4, with a little effort and practice you'll be able to get the maximum detail your camera is capable of delivering.

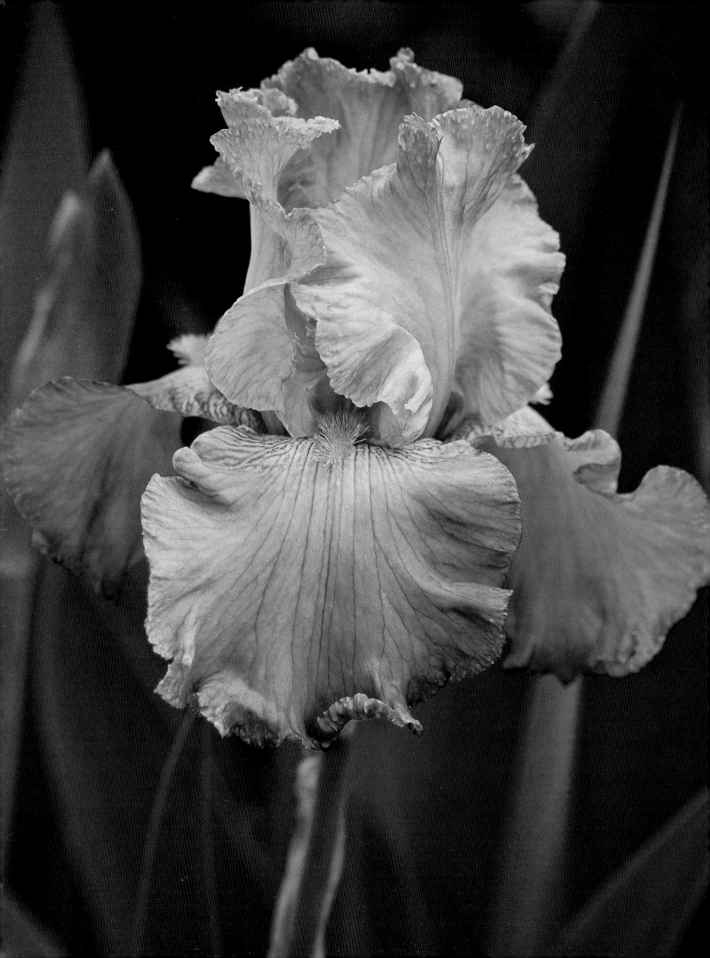

3

RAW CONVERSION

In chapter 2, I walked through the Adobe Camera Raw converter and its options. In this chapter, I'll expand on how to use those controls by providing numerous examples to give you a better understanding of how the controls respond. Mastery of these controls will give you the best possible image after conversion and minimize the amount of post-processing work you'll need to do.

- **Setting white balance**

- **Using the exposure control**

- **Using the blacks control**

- **Using the brightness control**

- **Using the contrast control**

- **Adjusting saturation**

- **Setting sharpness**

SETTING WHITE BALANCE

Unlike film, which is intended for specific lighting such as daylight or tungsten, digital media can be used in any light source by selecting the proper white balance, or color temperature, of the light used. Getting an accurate white balance can be a challenge, though, when shooting under different conditions.

The human eye does a great job of compensating for different lighting conditions. Regardless of what the light source is—incandescent, fluorescent, daylight, or firelight—we automatically adjust to see white as white.

Cameras, on the other hand, are very literal. They see exactly what shade of white is in the scene based on the lighting used. For incandescent, or firelight, situations, white is going to be seen with an orange or red tone. Fluorescent lighting will give that same white a greenish tint. This is because different light sources put out different color temperatures.

One advantage to shooting in digital is that color-temperature can be adjusted for each shot if needed. With film, color-compensation filters or lighting changes are required to change the way it responds to light since the entire roll of film will react to light in the same way. Film is typically balanced for daylight or tungsten lighting. Using daylight-balanced film under tungsten lighting, such as that which comes from the common light bulb, will result in photos with a strong orange or amber tone. To compensate using traditional methods, you can use an 80A (blue) filter when shooting in these conditions; tungsten film in daylight can be corrected with the 85A (amber) filter. Fluorescent lighting, thanks to its variety of color temperatures, can be corrected with either an FL-D or FL-B (magenta or amber) filter. All of this makes the ability of digital to set color temperature for individual situations without dealing with filters or film types very attractive. The adjustment to color temperature is referred to as "setting the white balance."

All digital cameras offer automatic white balance. Most offer several different preset white balance settings as well, such as Cloudy, Tungsten, Fluorescent, Daylight, and Flash. Some of the more pro-oriented cameras will allow you to set the white balance to a specific temperature setting.

In general, the Auto setting works well, especially when shooting RAW. Since the actual white balance isn't being applied to the RAW image, it's easy to change this after the fact in Adobe Camera Raw.

NOTE: Which adjustment first? I usually prefer to make white balance adjustments before using any of the other adjustment controls in Camera Raw. The one exception is when the exposure is way off. This is a good general rule to follow.

White balance and exposure will be the first two adjustments made to an image. Correct the one that is furthest from accurate first. Shadows, brightness, and contrast will follow these adjustments. Again, if brightness or contrast is way off, make adjustments to those settings first and then adjust the shadows.

As you make adjustments, you will likely find yourself going back to fine-tune the other sliders. RAW image conversion is often an "iterative" process, with each slider affecting the other. When making adjustments, I will often go back and fine-tune a slider setting based on another adjustment. For example, I'll start by making an adjustment to Exposure. An adjustment to Blacks or Recovery might require me to go back to the Exposure slider and make a minor change to my original adjustment to have the perfect combination of adjustments.

Using White Balance Presets

Adobe Camera Raw includes all of the common white-balance presets. If you know that a particular image was shot under one of these lighting conditions, correction can be as simple as a selection from the list. I find that these presets do a good job of getting me close to the white balance I want, but they seldom hit exactly on the right color.

The presets, as seen in **FIGURE 3.1**, include all of the common lighting conditions as well as three additional choices:

> As Shot will use the setting from your camera if Camera Raw can read it. This is most useful if you've set a custom white balance in the camera.

> Auto will attempt to correct the color balance to what Camera Raw thinks is correct. Camera Raw analyzes the image and makes a best guess at the correct white balance.

> Custom will be used whenever any adjustment is made to the Temperature or Tint sliders.

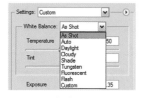

FIGURE 3.1 The list of preset white balance options in Adobe Camera Raw serves as a good starting point for making adjustments to your images.

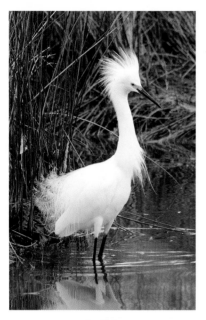
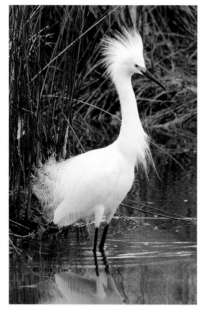
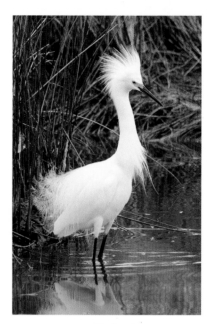

| Daylight | Cloudy | Shade |

FIGURE 3.2 This series of images, all conversions of the same shot, show how different white-balance settings can be between Daylight, Cloudy, Shade—all possible options for this particular image. The first example is with the Daylight setting of 5500. The Cloudy preset, with a setting of 6500, has a much warmer tone. The Shade preset, at 7500, is warmer yet; this one is obviously off, with much more yellow than I want.

FIGURE 3.2 shows the same outdoor image using different white balance presets. Any one of them could be correct depending on the light and look I want to convey, but each is very different from the other.

Which is correct? I know from the shooting conditions that the Daylight setting is the closest to correct, but otherwise I would have a hard time deciding which was technically correct. Although Daylight is the closest setting to what I want, it isn't exactly what I'm looking for. By using the Temperature and Tint controls, you can adjust the white balance to the correct setting for that image.

Using the Temperature and Tint Controls

You can fine-tune the color balance with the Temperature and Tint sliders. The Temperature slider displays the current color temperature in Kelvin, with lower numbers having more yellow and higher numbers having more blue. The control ranges from 2000, which is very yellow, to 50,000, or very blue. It would be unusual to have an image that comes anywhere near the upper end of the scale, but the lower end is about the same as a dim candle.

The Tint slider is used to adjust the magenta and green tones in the image. Moving the slider to the left, or to negative numbers, increases the amount of green, whereas positive adjustments to the right increases the magenta in your image.

Starting with the same image used in the earlier example, **FIGURE 3.3** shows the final image with the white balance fine-tuned. To reach the exact setting I was looking for, I chose the Daylight setting from the preset White Balance list; it was close but still a bit too warm. By moving the Temperature slider down to 4650, the white balance was corrected.

NOTE: Wait a second! If cooler temperatures are higher numbers, why do you raise the temperature setting to warm up an image? Good question, and I'm glad you asked! Adjustments to the temperature slider are actually compensating for the color temperature of the image. So if you move the slider to the left, you are adding blue to correct for the existing yellow light.

The Tint slider has an obvious use, but it can also be used for creative techniques, such as toning images to emulate alternative processing, which I'll show you in chapter 4.

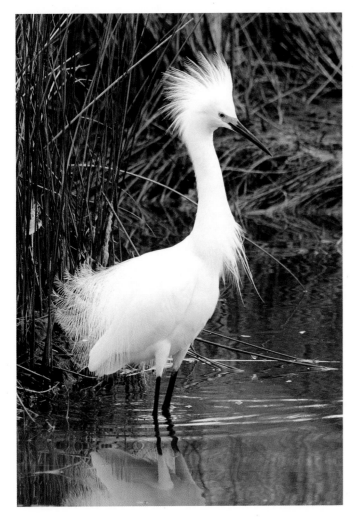

FIGURE 3.3 I started with the Daylight setting, which was closest to correct, and then adjusted the temperature slider until I ended up with this exposure, which has the color balance I remember from the scene. The final setting for the image was 4650.

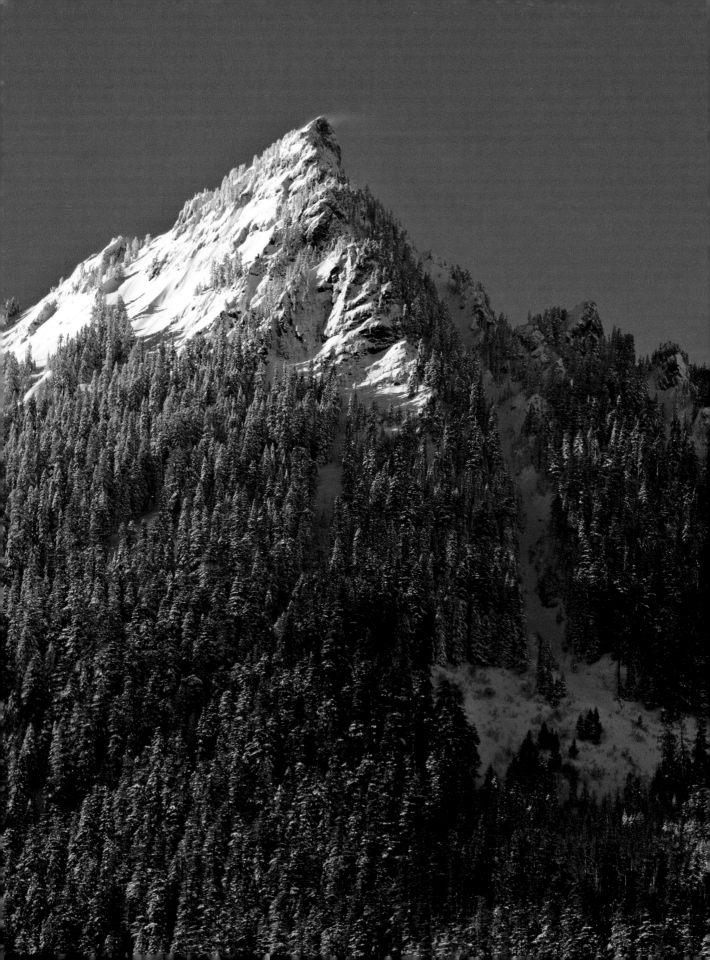

USING THE EXPOSURE CONTROL

The Exposure slider works like the exposure compensation setting on your camera. The numbers shown are equivalent to *f*-stops, with higher numbers adding more light to the scene and negative numbers subtracting light. The slider has a range of four stops in either direction, which gives you a great deal of control over the image after the capture. If you've used the Levels command in Photoshop Elements or Photoshop, the Exposure control is similar in function to the far right, or white point, slider. However, the Exposure control in Camera Raw is much more powerful than a simple white-point adjustment in the Levels command, as you'll see here.

NOTE: Seldom will you make only a single adjustment in Camera Raw. Adjustments to Exposure typically lead to adjustments in the other controls as well. The following examples are typical of the steps involved in correcting exposure.

I spend more time explaining exposure than any of the other topics in this chapter because exposure is critical to the quality of a converted image and is the most powerful control in Adobe Camera Raw, allowing you to perform either miracles or digital assault-and-battery on your images.

Correcting Underexposure

In the typical image, you'll be adjusting the exposure to bring the white point of the image to the far right of the histogram. For underexposed images, such as the one in **FIGURE 3.4**, you can add exposure by moving the slider to the right.

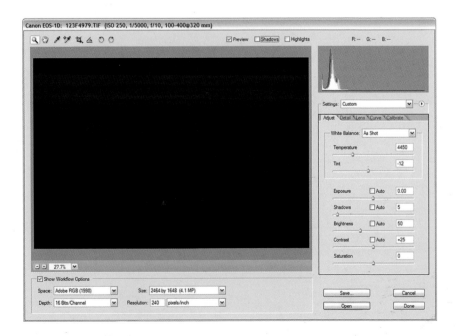

FIGURE 3.4 The original RAW image is underexposed. Had this been a JPEG file, the amount of detail recoverable would have made this image unusable.

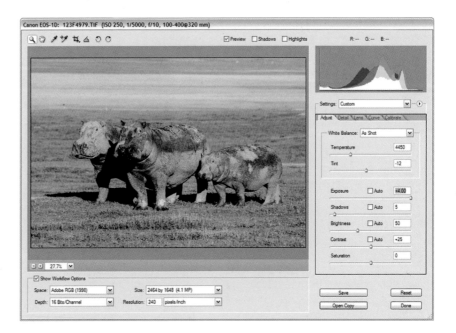

FIGURE 3.5 Adjusting the Exposure control results in a display of detail across the histogram.

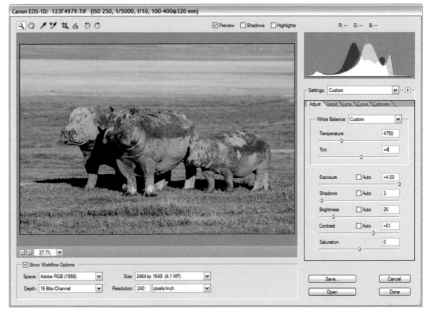

FIGURE 3.6 Additional adjustments made to shadows, brightness, contrast, and white balance have corrected the image further. Note that the histogram is more evenly distributed from shadow to highlight.

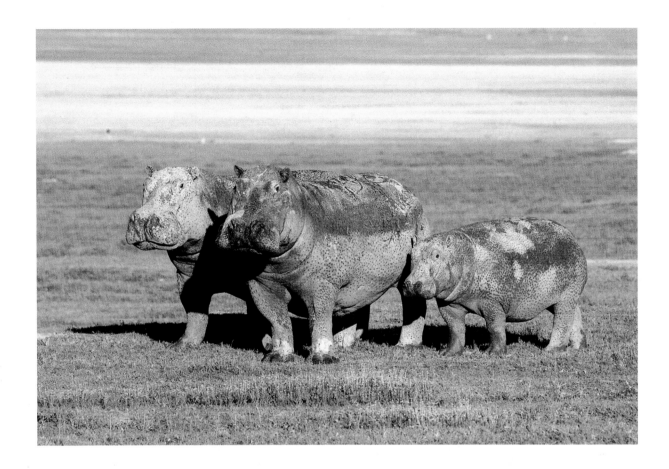

As you can see, the histogram is compressed well to the left, or shadow side. To begin the correction, you'll drag the Exposure slider to the right. For this particular image, even a full four stops doesn't begin to clip the highlights, but, as you can see from **FIGURE 3.5**, it has made a huge difference in the amount of detail available.

Further adjustments to the other sliders in Camera Raw fine-tune the image for shadow and contrast. Adjustments to both the Temperature and Tint controls correct the colorcast and white-balance problems in the original image, as seen in **FIGURE 3.6**.

The final image, shown in **FIGURE 3.7**, is now very usable because of the latitude offered by the RAW format.

FIGURE 3.7 Shooting in RAW gave this image a new lease on life. No other format would have allowed such drastic editing. (Courtesy Art Morris, www.birdsasart.com)

NOTE: Don't forget the Alt/Option key and slider adjustment combo that changes the preview display to help you determine highlight problems when making Exposure adjustments. Holding the key down while dragging the Shadows slider will turn the preview area into a clipping display.

Correcting Overexposure

Where Camera Raw really excels with exposure correction is in overexposure. Unlike conventional tools, such as the Levels command, Camera Raw can recover highlight detail with a much greater amount of control. In fact, if there is still image data in even one color channel, Camera Raw can recover that detail. Of course, the more color channels that contain data the better the recovery will be, but it's pretty impressive to see how much can be gained from even one channel. **FIGURE 3.8** shows an image that is overexposed in the clouds. Notice that the histogram is showing a spike on the right, or highlight, side and mostly in the blue channel.

I start off by moving the Exposure slider to the left, taking away light from the image. At -0.60, the highlights are no longer clipped. I can verify this by holding down the Alt/Option key while clicking the Exposure slider, which shows that no data is being clipped. **FIGURE 3.9** shows the image after adjusting the exposure.

As with the underexposed image in the previous example, adjustments are made to the Shadow, Brightness, Contrast, and Temperature sliders to finish the correction. The final image, shown in **FIGURE 3.10**, is significantly better in both tonal range and detail.

The end image shown in **FIGURE 3.11** is now much better than the original RAW file. While this isn't as extreme of an example as the underexposed image, had this been a JPEG file to begin with, I would not have been able to recover the highlight detail in the clouds.

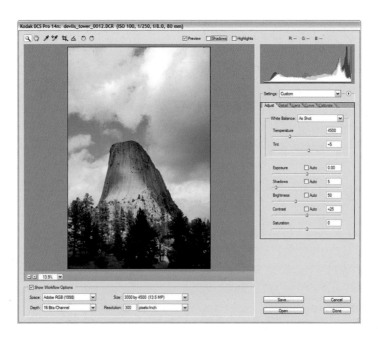

FIGURE 3.8 An overexposed image with loss of detail in the clouds. To correct this, the Exposure slider needs to be moved to the left.

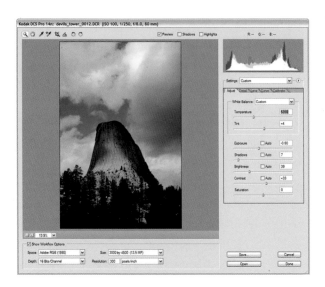

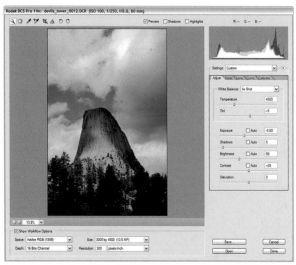

FIGURE 3.9 After lowering the exposure by almost two thirds of a stop, the highlights have moved within range and more detail is visible in the clouds.

FIGURE 3.10 The final image settings are made to correct shadow and contrast along with color balance. The histogram is now much more evenly distributed.

FIGURE 3.11 The final image corrected. Notice the additional detail in the highlights as well as the stronger shadow areas.

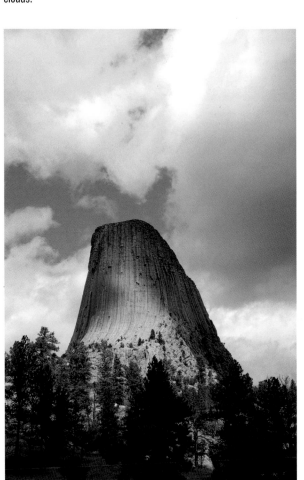

The next example shows how well Camera Raw can recover detail in what looks like a hopelessly overexposed image. **FIGURE 3.12** shows the starting image: a leaf in snow. I shot this without noticing that the camera was still set to manual exposure. The first lesson learned: 1/60 second at *f*5.6 isn't the right exposure for bright sun and snow!

You can see from the histogram that most of the image is against the right side. I turned off clipping highlights for a better view of the image. With the highlights box checked, everything in the image except the leaf is red.

The first step is to make exposure corrections to see if there is anything that can be recovered. I ended up subtracting almost 2.5 stops of exposure to the image, as shown in **FIGURE 3.13**, but did recover significant amounts of detail in the snow and fixed the exposure for the leaf quite nicely.

After setting the white balance and adjusting the tint to remove the magenta cast, adjustments to shadows were made, as well as a bit more tweaking to the exposure control. Finally, I adjusted brightness and contrast to arrive at **FIGURE 3.14**.

After opening the image in Photoshop, I did a little cleaning up around the leaf and decided to add some punch to the image by changing the color of the leaf to red. **FIGURE 3.15** shows the end image. There are still blown highlights in the image—Photoshop couldn't completely save me from myself—but the image is vastly better than the original, thanks to the latitude that shooting in RAW provides.

FIGURE 3.12 The starting image is grossly overexposed. Had this been a JPEG file, it would already be in the trash.

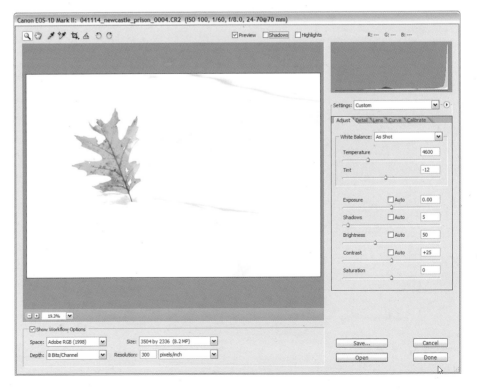

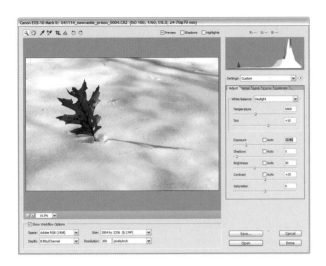

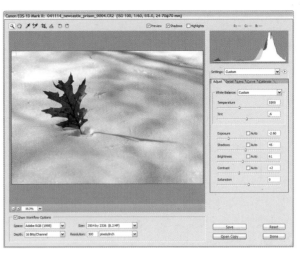

FIGURE 3.13 I made a −2.4 adjustment to exposure here, which helped significantly. Since the white balance was off, I set this to Daylight, but you can see that the tint is now off.

FIGURE 3.14 With some adjustments to the other controls in Camera Raw, the image looks much better, and the histogram is now more evenly distributed, with values from shadow to highlight.

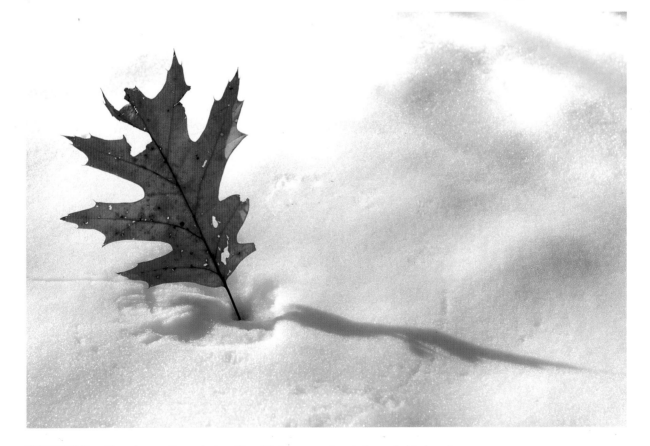

FIGURE 3.15 Not willing to leave well enough alone, I found that some cropping, cloning, and a bit of creative leaf coloring resulted in an image that is much better than the one I started with.

USING THE BLACKS CONTROL

The Shadows slider is similar to the slider in the Levels command that is used to set the black point of the image, or at that point in the image in which all detail is lost and pixel values are pure black. The control works by stretching the shadow values in your image. By moving the slider to the right, the number of pixels that are mapped to black increases, which can also give the appearance of increased contrast. Although the control ranges from 0 to 100, typical settings for the Shadows slider will be low—often less than 10. As with the Exposure control, the best method of using the Shadows control is by checking the clipping checkbox for telltale signs of loss of detail in the shadows. Keep a close eye on the left side of the histogram as you make your adjustments to prevent more data from being clipped than you want.

Fine-Tuning the Shadows

With the Shadows control, I prefer to leave a bit of extra space to allow for curves and other adjustments after the conversion process. **FIGURE 3.16** shows an image for which using the Auto checkbox sets Shadows to 8. The histogram for the image looks pretty good, with image data contained within the boundaries of the histogram. You can see from the preview that some of the black in the egret's legs are showing in blue, indicating that shadow detail is being clipped.

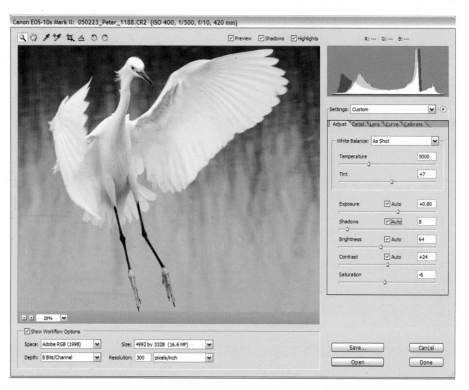

FIGURE 3.16 The automatic setting for Shadows in this image is 8. There is some clipping in the egret's legs, but this is acceptable for the subject.

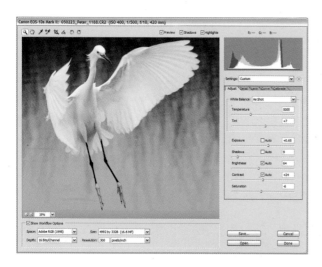

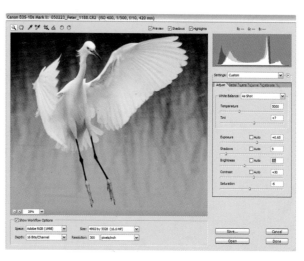

FIGURE 3.17 Dropping the exposure just enough to eliminate clipped highlights has given the image enough room to increase shadow detail by 1 point. It doesn't make a difference in the amount of shadow data being clipped, but it darkens the background a bit to make the bird stand out more.

FIGURE 3.18 After the exposure and shadows are adjusted, the Brightness control is reduced to eliminate highlight problems, and contrast is boosted a bit.

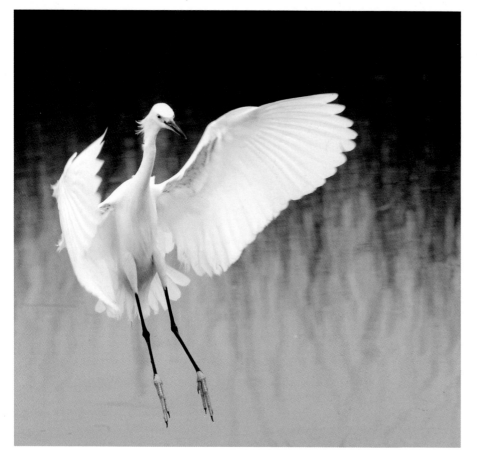

FIGURE 3.19 The converted image has better highlight detail and stands out from the background after the adjustments made in Camera Raw.

You can also see that a bit of highlight detail is being clipped at the top of the bird's head and wing. The first step in correcting the image is to reduce the exposure to bring the highlights into range, so I reduce the exposure setting to +.65. This lets me add just a bit more shadow detail to darken the background a bit. With just an increase of one, more shadow detail is also added to the egret's wings. **FIGURE 3.17** shows the new settings. Final adjustments are then made to Brightness and Contrast, as shown in **FIGURE 3.18**. The final image, shown in **FIGURE 3.19**, has better detail in both the shadows and highlights with more separation of the subject from the background than the RAW file originally had.

Making Larger Adjustments

The previous example only required minor changes to get the shadows where they belonged. Some images require more extensive changes to adjust the shadow detail properly. Because noise is more of a problem in the shadows, larger adjustments carry the risk of introducing noise into the image. To start off, the image in **FIGURE 3.20** needs a large adjustment to the shadows.

By increasing the Shadows slider to 34, as shown in **FIGURE 3.21**, the bird and fish both have better separation between shadows and mid-tones as well as from the blue sky.

The final result, shown in **FIGURE 3.22**, has excellent detail throughout the image, with fine shadows and highlights as well as mid-tones.

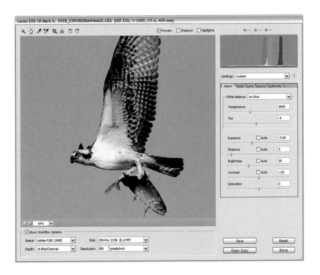

FIGURE 3.20 A more extreme example, this image could benefit from a large adjustment to the shadows.

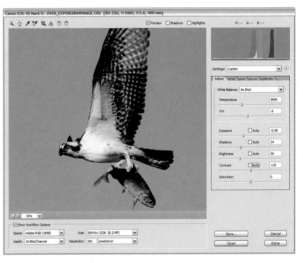

FIGURE 3.21 Increasing the Shadows slider to 34 provides much more detail and separation between shadow and mid-tone.

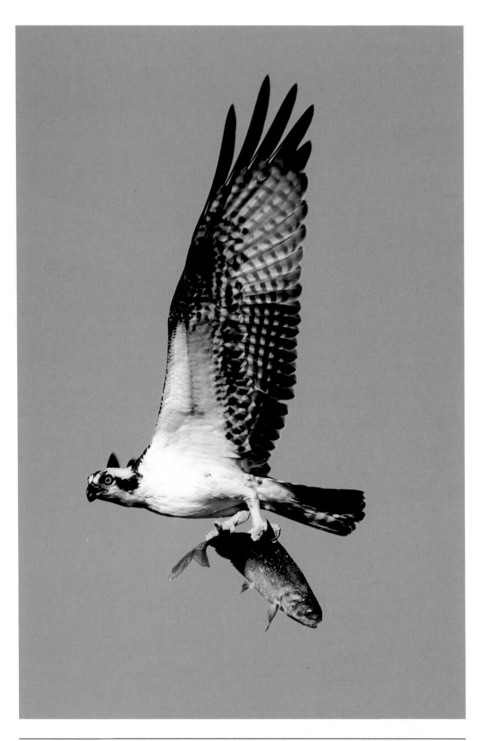

FIGURE 3.22 The converted image has excellent detail from shadow to highlight with the increased Shadows slider. (Image courtesy Art Morris, www.birdsasart.com)

NOTE: Don't forget the Alt-click/Option-click and slider-adjustment combo that changes the preview display to help you determine shadow problems when making shadow adjustments. Holding the key down while dragging the Shadows slider will turn the preview area into a clipping display.

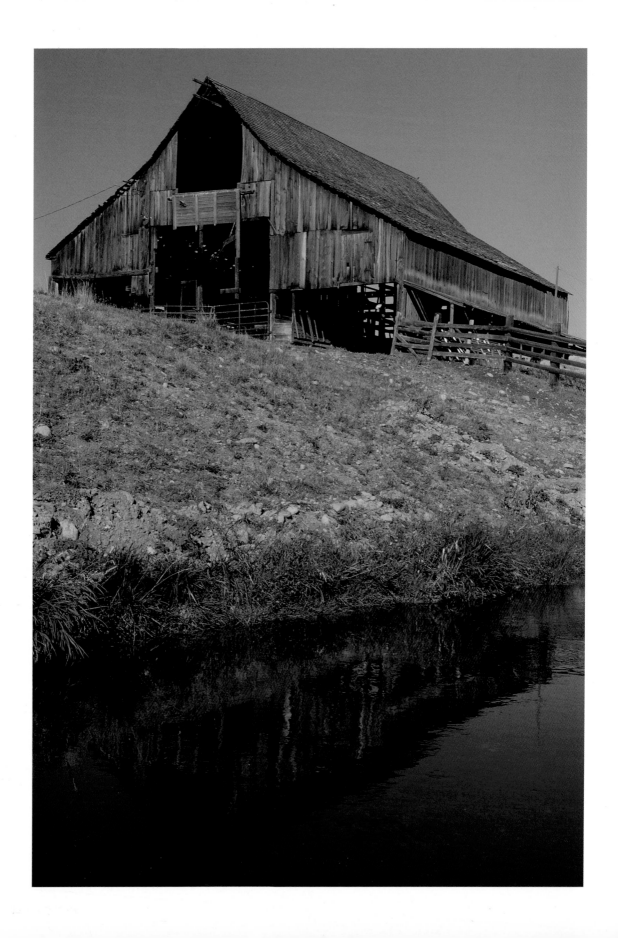

USING THE BRIGHTNESS CONTROL

Your first impression of the Brightness control might have you wondering what is different than the Exposure control. It does make similar adjustments, brightening or darkening the image, but rather than setting the black and white clipping points, the Brightness control works by compressing or expanding highlight and shadow detail.

NOTE: The Brightness control should be used *after* exposure and shadow adjustments have been made.

This is similar in function to the middle slider in the Photoshop Elements and Photoshop Levels dialog. The image in **FIGURE 3.23** will be used to show the effect of the Brightness control.

To make your image brighter overall, move the slider control to the left. This compresses the shadows while expanding the highlights. **FIGURE 3.24** shows the image after this adjustment. You can see by the histogram that the shadows have been reduced while more of the image data have moved into the center portion of the histogram. Most important, though, this has opened up the image enough so that detail is visible in the background wallpaper.

Like the other controls in Camera Raw, keep your eye on the histogram to see how the image data are adjusting. Extreme adjustments will clip highlight and shadow detail, so take it nice and easy as you correct your images.

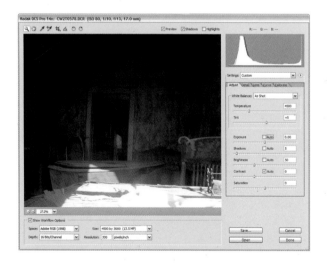 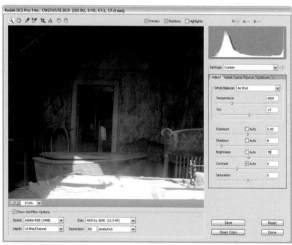

FIGURE 3.23 This is our starting point for making adjustments to the Brightness control.

FIGURE 3.24 After you adjust the Brightness control by moving the slider to the left, you will see more mid-tone in the image.

USING THE CONTRAST CONTROL

The Contrast control adjusts the mid-tones in an image. Photoshop Elements has a Levels control that works in a similar manner, while Photoshop users will likely be familiar with the Curves control, which is a more powerful adjustment tool. Like the Brightness control, Contrast should be adjusted after Exposure and Shadows and normally after Brightness.

Almost all RAW files will benefit from some contrast adjustment. Some images, such as portraits, particularly of women, will use a lower setting

---

NOTE: I'll cover the Curves control included with Photoshop CS4's version of Camera Raw in chapter 6.

NOTE: For more detailed information on Curves and Levels, I recommend *Photoshop CS4 Workflow* by Tim Grey or *Photoshop for Nature Photographers* by Ellen Anon.

To increase the contrast in a RAW file, adjust the Contrast slider to the left. Moving the slider to the right decreases contrast in the image, giving it a flatter look. In **FIGURE 3.25**, the Auto setting of +19 was too strong for this image, creating harsh shadows on the model's face, so I adjusted the Contrast slider to +3.

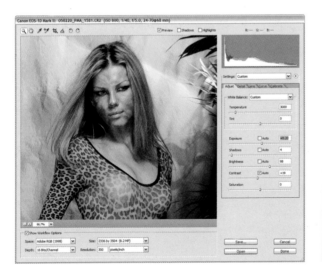 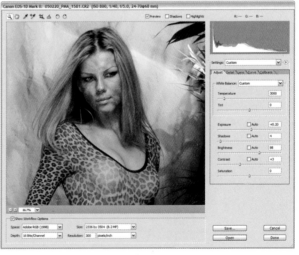

FIGURE 3.25 *Left*: The default setting for contrast on this image was too high with the mid-tones too strong on the model's face. *Right*: Lowering the contrast in Camera Raw corrected the problem.

In contrast to the previous image, the example shown in **FIGURE 3.26** needed an increase in contrast. The original was a bit flat, with no real definition from shadow to mid-tone. By increasing the Contrast slider to 52, the image has a more dramatic look.

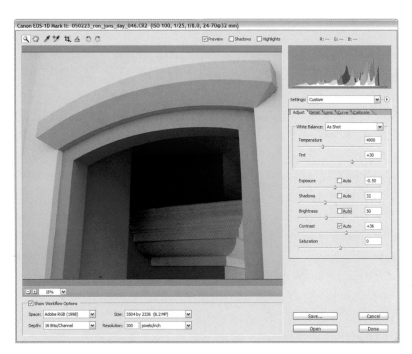

FIGURE 3.26 *Top*: The default setting for contrast on this image was too low and the entire image looks rather flat. *Bottom*: Raising the contrast in Camera Raw corrected the problem.

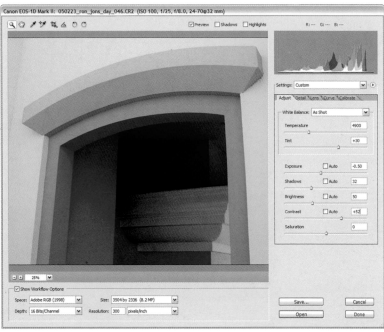

SETTING SHARPNESS

Although Camera Raw includes a Sharpness slider, applying sharpening during the conversion is not the ideal method to use. Since sharpening needs will be specific to each image and the intended output, setting default sharpness can lead to problems after the conversion.

The problem with turning sharpening off, though, is that your image will appear somewhat soft when displayed in Camera Raw. The best way to deal with this is to use the Sharpness slider only on the preview image.

Photoshop CS4 allows you to apply sharpening to the preview only in the Preferences dialog. This will let you see how your image will look with sharpening applied, but when the conversion is done, it will not affect the converted image. To set Camera Raw to use sharpening only on the preview, select Preferences from the pull-down menu next to the Settings list. In the Camera Raw Preferences dialog, select Preview Images Only from the Apply Sharpening To list, as shown in **FIGURE 3.27**. Click OK to save your changes and return to Camera Raw.

Photoshop Elements users don't have this advantage, since the version of Camera Raw included in Elements doesn't have a Preferences option. For users of this version, the safest method is to leave the Sharpness slider set to 0. You can make this the default for Camera Raw by setting the slider to 0 and selecting Set Camera Default from the settings menu.

NOTE: As an alternative, you can use the control during the editing phase and then set to 0 before converting. My memory doesn't always remind me to do this, though. The good news is that you can always reconvert the image if needed—yet another reason to love RAW!

I'll cover the basics of post-conversion sharpening in chapter 7, along with the other common post-conversion options, such as resizing and saving your images.

FIGURE 3.27 To prevent your converted files from having the Sharpness setting applied, select Apply sharpening to Preview images only in the Preferences dialog.

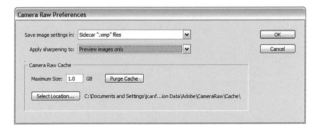

ADJUSTING SATURATION: NOT YET

When beginning to work with RAW images, many people are surprised at how flat the images look when compared to the JPEGs they have been shooting. The primary reason for this is that JPEG images are already converted when you see them. The camera has made decisions on how much saturation to apply, and more often than not it tends to make your images more saturated because the eye is more easily drawn to rich color.

If saturation needs to be adjusted, I usually prefer to make these adjustments after the conversion using the tools in Photoshop, which give greater control over the process. If adjustments are to be made in Camera Raw, they should be minimal. There is one exception to this, though, and it's one that not many people consider-black-and-white conversion in Camera Raw. I'll cover this technique in detail in chapter 4.

SUMMARY

Knowing what each of the controls in Adobe Camera Raw does and how they interact with each other is a critical part of the RAW workflow. Camera Raw will allow you to make adjustments to your images that would be impossible or extremely difficult in Photoshop Elements or Photoshop CS. Best of all, it makes these adjustments using all the data stored in your RAW file. If you decide you don't like the settings after your conversion, the original RAW file is still available to you, ready for the next experiment.

Along with an understanding of how each of the controls work, I hope you have come to appreciate what an important tool the histogram is.

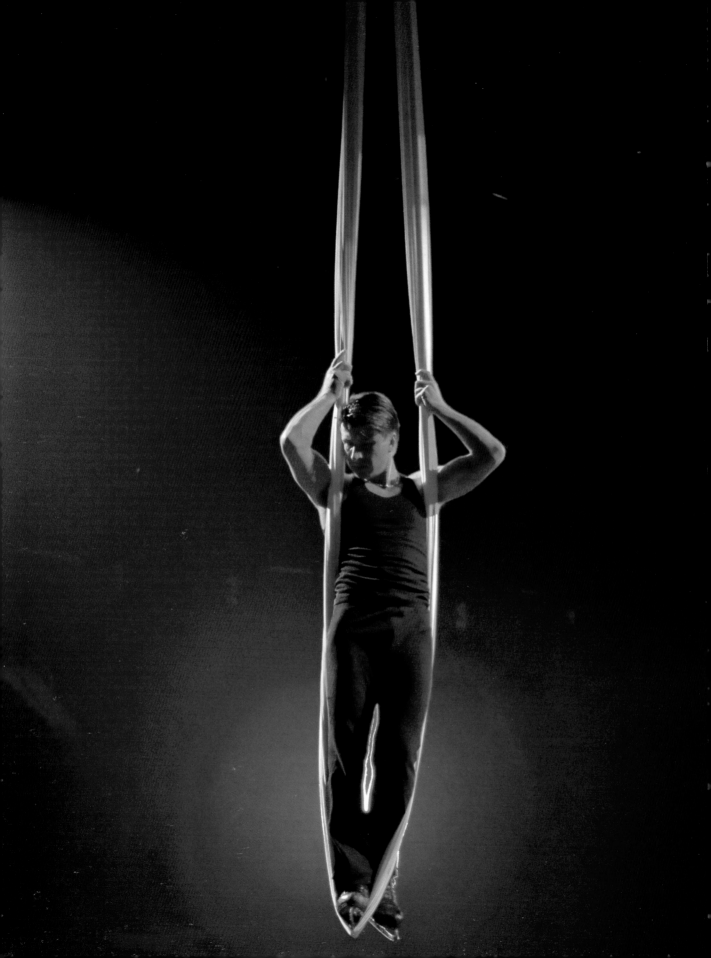

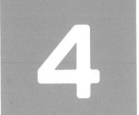

BEYOND THE BASICS

Now that you have a good understanding of how the major adjustment controls work in Adobe Camera Raw, you're ready to go beyond the basic RAW file conversion and start to tap in to the extra power you have with the Camera Raw converter. Using the controls covered in this chapter, you'll be able to tone images, reduce noise problems, and do very good black-and-white conversions— all using all the data in your RAW file. If you find yourself using certain settings frequently, you'll appreciate knowing how to save and use custom settings to accelerate your workflow.

- **Using the white balance tool**

- **Adjusting color tint**

- **Controlling noise with Luminance Smoothing**

- **Controlling noise with Color Noise Reduction**

- **Converting to black and white**

- **Saving and using custom settings**

USING THE WHITE BALANCE TOOL

The White Balance tool ✒ in Adobe Camera Raw works differently than the other white eyedroppers in Photoshop Elements and Photoshop. Rather than sample the color you click (as the eyedropper in the Tool palette does) or set a white point (like the white eyedropper in the Levels and Curves commands), the eyedropper in Camera Raw sets the white balance of the image based on where you click, which is how the center, or gray, eyedropper works. In other words, wherever you click the white balance eyedropper in Camera Raw, all three color channels will be set to the same value, making that the neutral reference for your image. When you click a point in your image, that point determines the color temperature and tint of your image by measuring the color values of the pixels under the eyedropper. The White Balance tool works best on any areas of the image that still contain detail and would look correct if made to be neutral in tone. **FIGURE 4.1** shows the difference between clicking a highlight area with no detail and clicking one with some detail.

When you have several possible areas in your image that could be used to set white balance (as shown in **FIGURE 4.2**), click each of them to see which selection gives you the temperature and tint you're looking for. Remember that photography is subjective, and within reason there can be multiple correct choices.

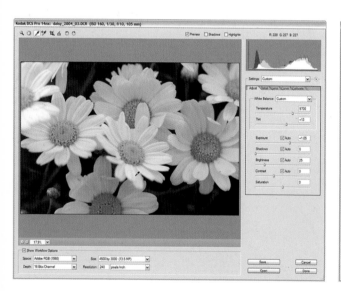 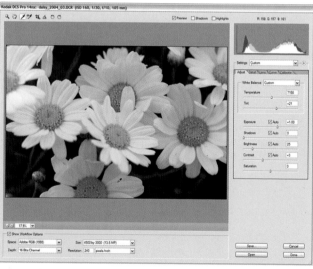

FIGURE 4.1 The White Balance tool in Camera Raw works by setting the temperature and tint of the image based on the point you click. *Left:* Clicking a highlight area with no detail results in an image that is warmer. *Right:* When you select an area with some detail in the highlights, the color balance is rendered more accurately.

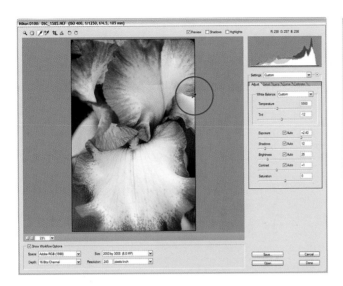
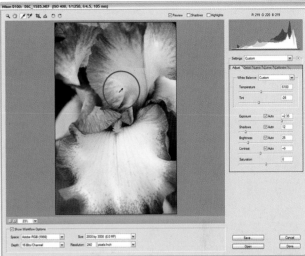
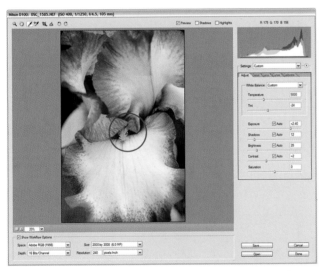
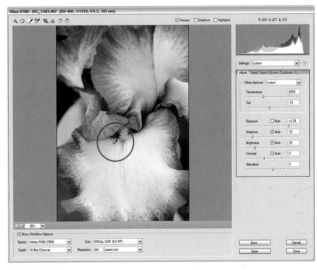

FIGURE 4.2 Variations on a theme. All four of these images use a different white balance as selected by the White Balance tool. Any of them could be considered correct, depending on the mood I want to convey. Which is best? You decide!

ADJUSTING COLOR TINT

The Tint slider in Adobe Camera Raw is commonly used to fine-tune the color of your images. By moving the slider to the left, more green is added to the image. Adjustments to the right add more magenta. You can also use the Tint slider for some creative effects. This works best with high-key images (ones that contain mostly highlights with little tone separation) and in conjunction with the Temperature slider when you want an alternate processing tone, such as platinum or sepia.

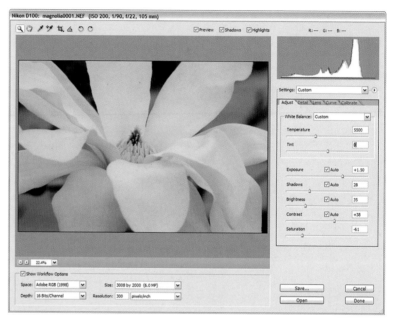

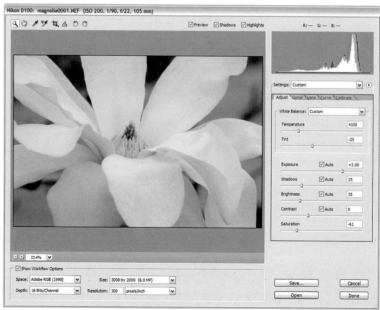

Starting with a high-key image open in Camera Raw, adjust the Tint slider in the direction you want the final image to go. To add blue or green tones, adjust to the left; to add reds and sepias, adjust the slider to the right. **FIGURE 4.3** shows an original as well as three alternately toned images.

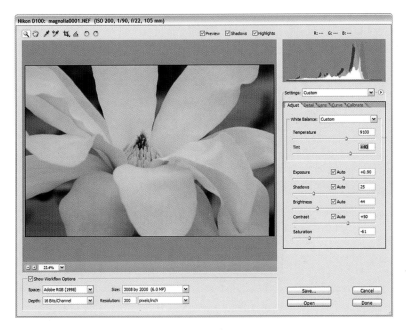

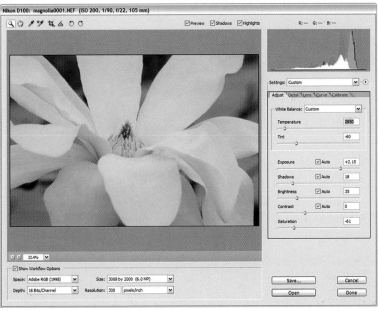

FIGURE 4.3 You can mimic alternative processing techniques with the Tint slider. This works best with high-key images that have little color variation to begin with. For these examples, I've used settings of 0 for the neutral print (*opposite, top*), -25 for the platinum tone (*opposite, bottom*), +40 for the sepia tone (*top*), and -60 for the selenium tone print (*bottom*). In all cases, the adjustment was a combination of color temperature and tint.

CONTROLLING NOISE WITH LUMINANCE SMOOTHING

Luminance Smoothing is used to control the noise that appears in some digital images, particularly at higher ISO settings or with long exposures. Luminance noise looks like variations in tone, particularly in the shadow areas of an image, reminding many people of the grain in film. Most images, particularly those shot at lower ISO settings or shorter exposure lengths, will not need any changes to Luminance Smoothing, so don't plan on applying this to every image you convert.

Using the Luminance Smoothing control is easy enough: Anything above 0 will begin to remove the random noise. (If you're using Photoshop, this slider is on the Camera Raw Details tab.) The drawback to the control is that some softness will be introduced to the image as part of the correction. To get started, I recommend zooming in to at least a 100 percent preview of the area you are most concerned about, as shown in **FIGURE 4.4**.

NOTE: With the Luminance Smoothing and Color Noise Reduction sliders, I suggest zooming in as much as possible to see just what the noise problems are and how much correction is needed to reduce them.

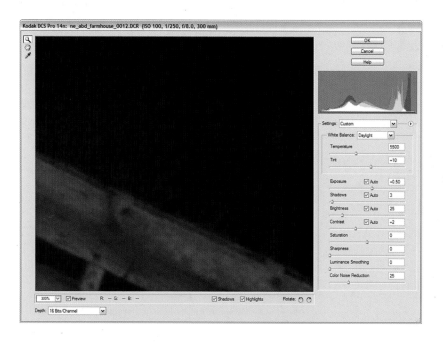

FIGURE 4.4 Zoom in as much as possible on the problem area before making Luminance Smoothing adjustments. Since this adjustment softens the image somewhat, you'll want to keep the changes to a minimum.

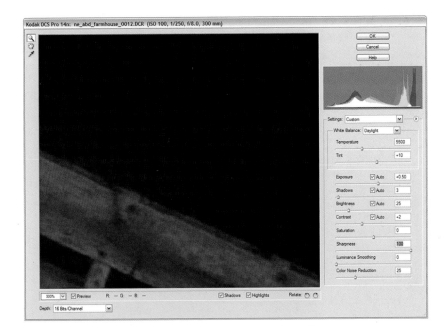

FIGURE 4.5 Applying sharpening to the image helps the luminance noise stand out more to help with editing.

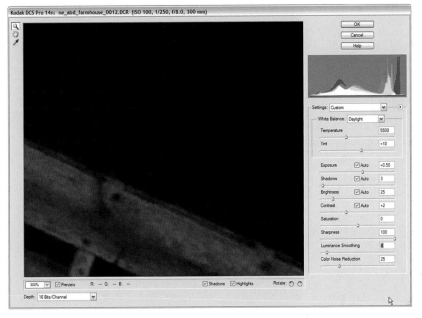

FIGURE 4.6 Increasing the Luminance Smoothing slider to a setting of 8 improves the appearance of noise.

NOTE: It may help to use the Sharpness slider to make the noise easier to detect (**FIG-URE 4.5**). If you do this, be sure to reset the slider to 0 before converting the RAW file.

I find that small adjustments here are normally the best, with many images requiring a value of less than 10, and very rarely up to 15. In the example in **FIGURE 4.6**, I've increased the setting to 8, which has reduced the appearance of noise, or graininess, in the image without destroying detail.

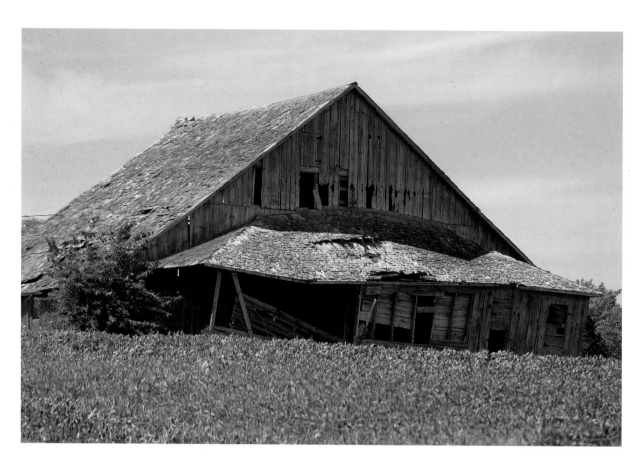

FIGURE 4.7 Before *(left)* and after *(right)* Luminance Smoothing. Note the differences in the shadow areas. The "after" image is smoother with fewer variations in tone.

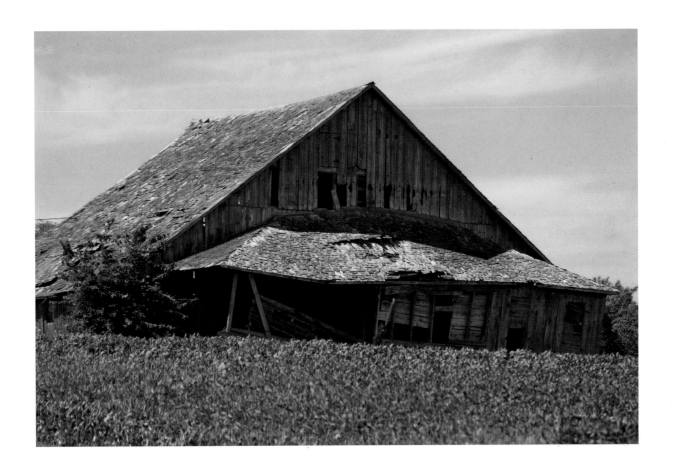

NOTE: If you are using Photoshop Elements, or you are using Photoshop and didn't take my advice in chapter 3 to apply sharpening to only the preview, be sure to return the Sharpness slider to 0 before converting the image.

Here's the converted image, without and with Luminance Smoothing applied. Compare the shadow areas of the image on the left with the same areas of the image on the right (**FIGURE 4.7**). There is less random variation in tone with the corrected image on the right. It's a subtle difference here, but in a larger print the change is very apparent.

CONTROLLING NOISE WITH COLOR NOISE REDUCTION

If you have green or magenta speckles in your image, particularly in dark areas, or you see these speckles around highlights in the image, you are a victim of color noise. This is more likely to occur with longer exposures and high ISO settings, and it shows up even more with high-resolution compact cameras that pack more photo sites (pixels) into a smaller area, resulting in sensors that are more sensitive to light than their digital SLR counterparts that use larger sensors.

The method of correcting color noise is very similar to the one used previously for luminance noise. Start off by zooming in as much as needed to see detail in the problem area of your image (**FIGURE 4.8**).

Color Noise Reduction doesn't have the same problem with affecting the sharpness of the converted image that Luminance Smoothing does, but you'll still want to keep your adjustments to the minimum acceptable here as well. (If you're using Photoshop, this slider is on the Camera Raw Details tab.) I suggest starting at the control's default setting of 25 and going from there. Again, watching the preview area as you make adjustments, look for the splotches of color to begin to blend away, as shown in **FIGURE 4.9**.

As you can see in the "before" and "after" (**FIGURE 4.10**) images, the green and magenta problem areas become much less visible in the shadows of the image with the adjustment.

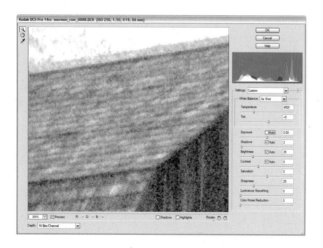

FIGURE 4.8 After zooming in on the problem area, the color-noise problems are obvious in this image. All of the green and magenta splotches are signs of noise.

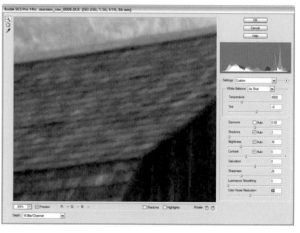

FIGURE 4.9 Moving the Color Noise Reduction slider to the right begins to blend the green and magenta color spots into the surrounding tones, making the image look less noisy. For this image, I've raised the slider to a setting of 42.

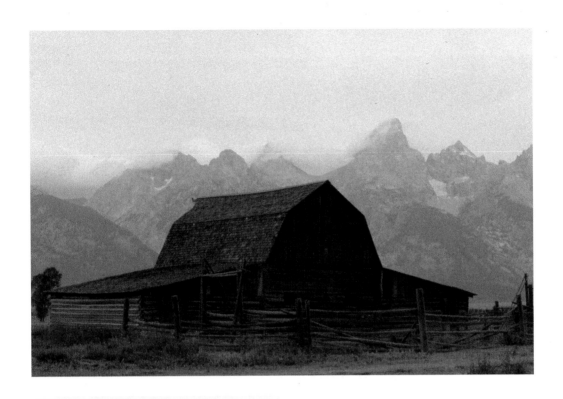

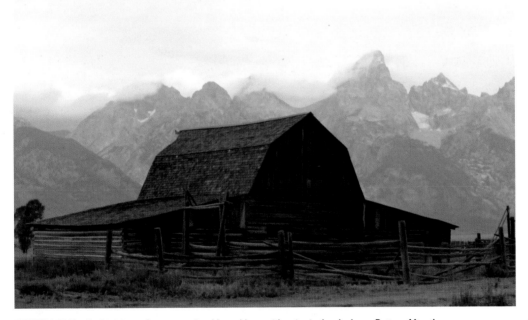

FIGURE 4.10 *Top*: In this image, there are noticeable problems with noise in the shadows. *Bottom*: After the noise-reduction slider is adjusted, the splotches of color are much less noticeable. This adjustment to noise reduction allowed other, minor adjustments to contrast and brightness to be made as well.

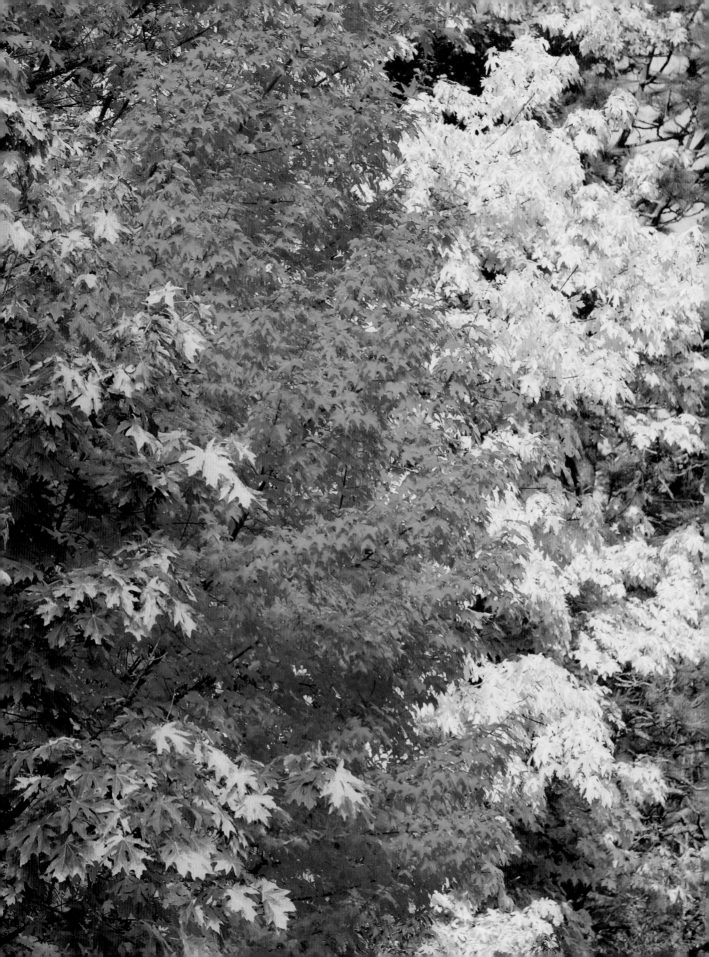

NOTE: WHEN TO LOOK INTO OTHER TOOLS

To be honest, the noise-reduction tools in Adobe Camera Raw don't offer the level of control that will take care of every noise problem you encounter. There are some other tools available that can work minor miracles on your noise-plagued images. However, these other tools have a couple of drawbacks that you should consider. First, it's an extra expense. Second, these programs don't work on the RAW images, so you'll need to do all your conversions first and then run the image, either a TIFF (recommended) or JPEG, through their noise-reduction process. Finally, it's an extra step in the workflow. With those caveats in mind, I recommend any of the following for those really tough noise problems. Each of the applications listed here works on both Macintosh OS X and Windows XP systems.

Noise Ninja (www.picturecode.com): This has both stand-alone and Photoshop and Photoshop Elements plug-in versions. The program includes numerous profiles for specific cameras and includes information on how to create your own profiles. Noise Ninja does the best job of luminance noise reduction of any program I've tried. I recommend getting the Pro version, which supports 16-bit images and batch-processing options. The Pro version costs about $79, which includes the plug-in and the stand-alone version.

nik Dfine (www.nikmultimedia.com, $99): This is a Photoshop and Photoshop Elements plug-in. Dfine has the most intuitive interface of all of the noise-reduction programs listed here and does a particularly good job with color-noise reduction. If you use any of the other nik products, such as Sharpener Pro or Color Efex, Dfine will be easy to understand and use.

Neat Image (www.neatimage.com): This is the other strong contender for noise reduction. Neat Image and Noise Ninja compete for best results on many images. Neat Image also has a stand-alone and plug-in version of the program. The stand-alone version supports batch processing and 16-bit files. It costs about $75 for the PC Pro bundle, which includes both versions, or $39.90 for the Mac version.

My Recommendation: If you frequently find yourself making adjustments to RAW images in Camera Raw but aren't happy with the results, take a look at one of the programs just described. All three work on Macintosh or Windows systems, and all work with Photoshop Elements and Photoshop. I recommend Noise Ninja. It does the best overall job and is significantly faster than the other options. All have free trial versions available, so try them out and see which suits your needs best.

CONVERTING TO BLACK AND WHITE

Black-and-white photography has become increasingly popular these days, in part due to the ease of converting digital images from color to grayscale. Image-editing programs, like Photoshop Elements and Photoshop, have always supported converting digital images to grayscale, although not always with the greatest results.

Black-and-White Images in Camera Raw

One of the best uses for the Saturation slider in Camera Raw is the conversion to black and white. By setting Saturation to –100, the image is displayed as grayscale. Converting in Camera Raw has its advantages: You have the full data from the RAW file to work with, and adjustments to exposure and shadow detail are better handled in Camera Raw than in Curves or Levels in Photoshop or Photoshop Elements after the conversion.

However, a simple saturation adjustment is seldom going to give you a good black-and-white image. In fact, desaturating a color image usually leaves you with a bland, flat-looking image. Most color images require a significant amount of "massaging" to turn them into a good black and white. Serious Photoshop users have learned to master the Channel Mixer control for their conversions, while Photoshop Elements and Photoshop users who deal with only black and white occasionally

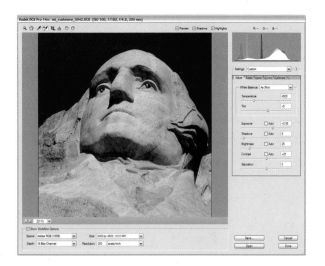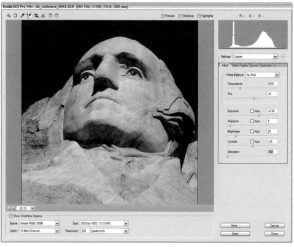

FIGURE 4.11 *Left:* This is the image I've selected to convert from color to black and white. *Right:* After setting the Saturation slider to the far left, I have a basic grayscale image.

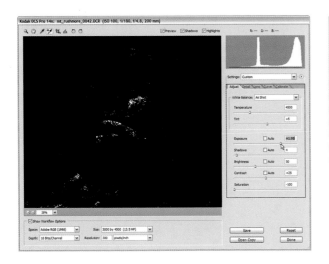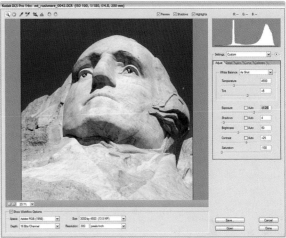

FIGURE 4.12 The next step is to adjust exposure to set the white values for the image. Start by identifying the critical highlight area of the image. This is the lightest area in which you want to retain image detail.

tend to go with one of the many plug-ins available. You can, however, do a very good job of black-and-white conversion within Camera Raw, and it's not as difficult as you might think.

To make this type of conversion, open a RAW image (**FIGURE 4.11**) and move the Saturation slider all the way to the left.

The next step is to make adjustments to exposure. Many black-and-white images look better with more defined white and black points. I find that adjusting the exposure for the maximum amount of highlight detail works best. To do this, first determine which highlight area in your image is the most important to retain detail in. This will serve as the guide for how much exposure you can add to the image. Using the Alt/Option key while adjusting the Exposure control, move the slider until you see the critical highlight area begin to clip, then back off the slider just enough to eliminate the clipping (**FIGURE 4.12**).

If you are using Photoshop, using the Color Sampler tool can help with this adjustment. Select the Color Sampler tool and click the highlight area you want to maintain. Now, when you adjust the exposure with the Alt/Option key, the sample point will be displayed while you make the adjustments so you'll know precisely where you were trying to keep detail (**FIGURE 4.13**).

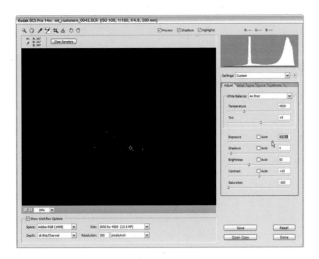

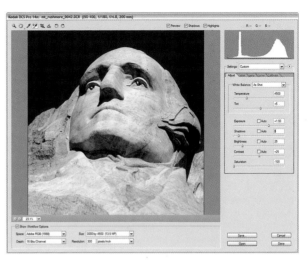

FIGURE 4.13 The Color Sampler tool in the Photoshop version of Camera Raw helps locate the highlight area while adjusting exposure.

FIGURE 4.14 After adjusting the Blacks slider to set the black values, the image is beginning to take on a more traditional black-and-white feel.

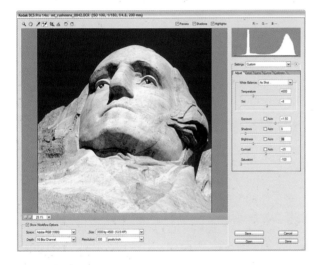

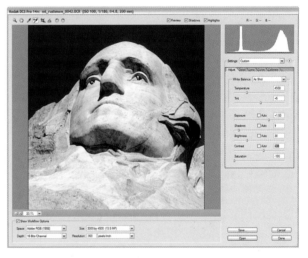

FIGURE 4.15 A small adjustment was made to the mid-tones with the Brightness slider.

FIGURE 4.16 Increasing the contrast will often add more depth to a black-and-white image.

Adjustments to the Blacks slider will set the black values for the image. Again using the Alt/Option key while making the adjustment, move the slider until you have the blacks set where you want them (**FIGURE 4.14**). As with the Exposure control, here you want to maintain detail in the important shadow area of your image.

Depending on the image and the amount of adjustment made to exposure, the Brightness slider may not need to be used at all. In **FIGURE 4.15**, I've made a small increase in overall brightness to open up the image a little more. This adjusts the mid-tones of the image and may or may not be appropriate for the type of image you are converting.

The final step in the conversion is to adjust contrast. Black-and-white images often need a boost in contrast when compared to the same image in color. In the example image shown in **FIGURE 4.16**, I've increased contrast to 38. The final version with contrast adjustments, shown in **FIGURE 4.17** on the right, is now ready for conversion. For a strong black-and-white image with good definition between tones, an increase in the Contrast slider can make a huge difference.

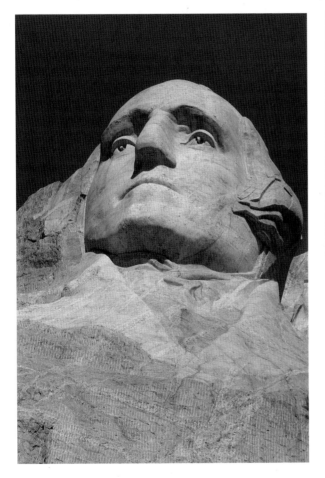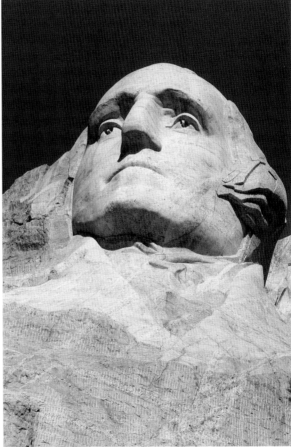

FIGURE 4.17 The image after only desaturation *(left)* looks very flat in comparison to the final image *(right)* with further adjustments in Camera Raw.

Advanced Black and White with Calibrate

If you are using Camera Raw with Photoshop, you have even more options available to you. The Calibrate tab can be used in a similar fashion as the Channel Mixer command in Photoshop. You'll start out the same way you did in the previous example, by reducing the Saturation to 0. After making adjustments to the major adjustment controls, you can fine-tune the black-and-white effect by using the Calibrate sliders.

Next, select the Calibrate tab in Camera Raw. The Red, Green, and Blue Hue

FIGURE 4.18 *Top*: The image prior to adjustments of the Hue and Saturation sliders. *Bottom*: Increasing the Red sliders enhances the rocks and adds contrast to the sky.

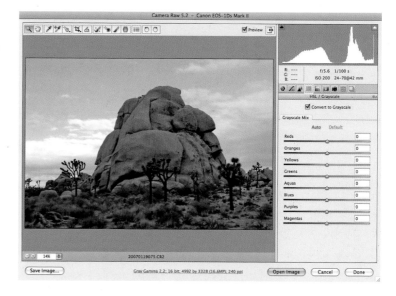

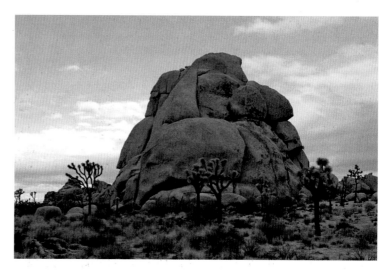

sliders work like the corresponding controls in the Channel Mixer control, while the Saturation sliders affect the intensity of the Hue sliders. While traditional black-and-white filters affect the opposite color, Calibrate's adjustments affect the color selected. For example, boosting the Red sliders, as shown in **FIGURE 4.18**, will darken reds in the image.

Increasing the Greens adds more intensity to green shades, as shown in **FIGURE 4.19**, while increasing the Blues to the values shown in **FIGURE 4.20** will darken the sky.

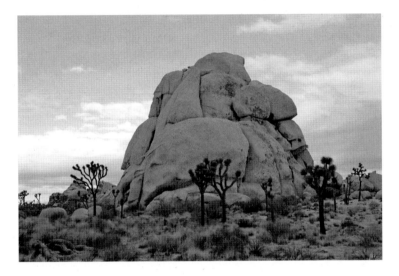

FIGURE 4.19 The image after adjusting the Green sliders to darken the trees.

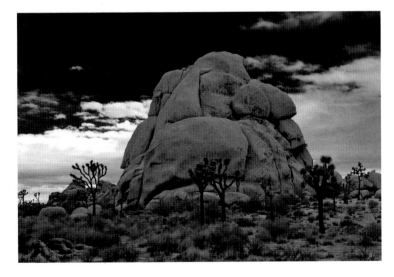

FIGURE 4.20 The Blue sliders have been adjusted up, which has darkened the sky and given the foreground subject more emphasis.

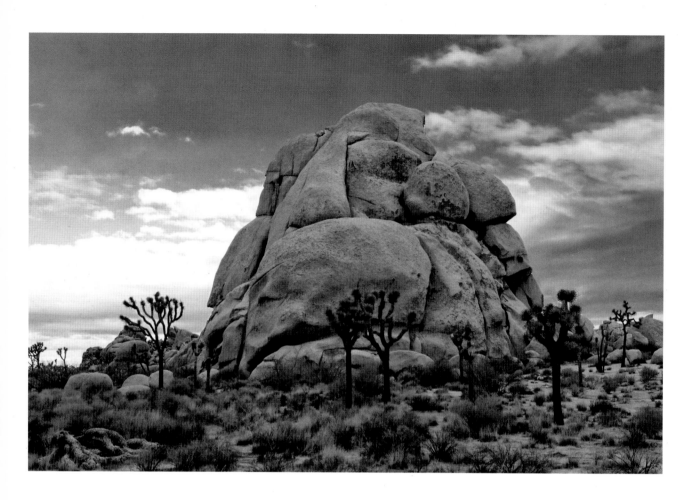

FIGURE 4.21 Here's the final image after cropping and sharpening in Photoshop. Much better than a simple grayscale conversion!

SAVING AND USING CUSTOM SETTINGS

Depending on which version of Camera Raw you are using, you can save or reset only the Camera Defaults or a wide range of individual options. Photoshop Elements only lets you save all of your adjustments. If you find that you are making the same adjustments to every, or nearly every, image you convert, you can save steps by making these settings the Camera Default (**FIGURE 4.22**). After making adjustments to the sliders, click the triangle next to the Settings drop-down list and choose Set Camera Default. These settings will now be used as the starting point for any new RAW image conversion.

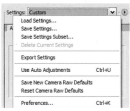

NOTE: You can return to the original settings by choosing Reset Camera Default from the Settings menu.

FIGURE 4.22 *Top*: Camera Raw in Photoshop Elements only gives you the option to set or reset the default settings. *Bottom*: Camera Raw in Photoshop offers a number of other options, including the ability to load and use a subset of the saved settings.

Since the camera default affects every setting in Camera Raw in Photoshop Elements, it is most useful when you have a group of images to convert with similar corrections. By correcting the first image, then saving the camera default, you can make the change once. Now, all future images opened will use the adjusted controls.

If you find that images from your camera consistently need corrections in luminance smoothing or color-noise reduction, making just those adjustments and saving the camera default will apply the new setting to future images.

Photoshop users of Camera Raw have significantly more options available to them than do users of Photoshop Elements. The ability to save and use subsets of the controls in this version of Camera Raw gives you the ability to create settings that are tuned to specific needs, such as a lens or custom color calibration. These techniques are covered in detail in chapter 6.

SUMMARY

This chapter has shown you how to fine-tune your image in Camera Raw to correct color balance and noise problems that may exist in the RAW file. Along the way, you've learned how to save custom settings to make recurring adjustments happen automatically. And, you've seen that Camera Raw can act as a high-quality black-and-white image-conversion program for your RAW images as well. In the next chapter, I'll show you how to put Camera Raw to work for you by automating many of these tasks.

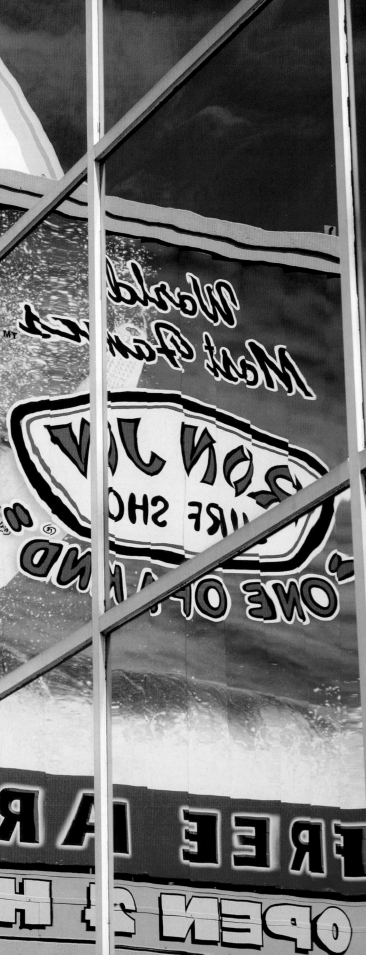
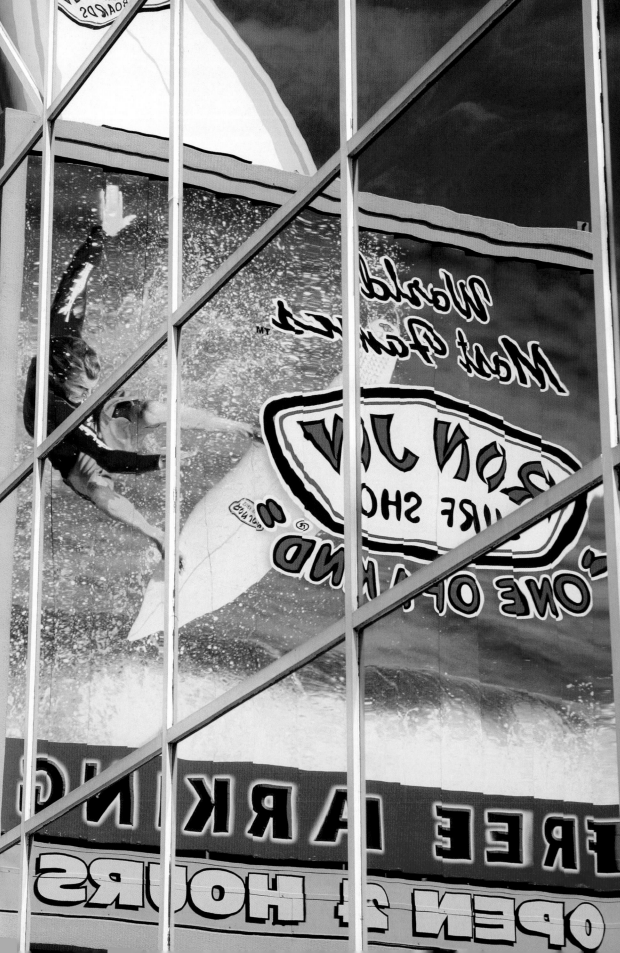

AUTOMATING CAMERA RAW

When you're looking at hundreds of RAW images, or even just a few, the thought of adjusting and converting each of them can be discouraging. Luckily, Adobe Camera Raw has several options available for automating the task. In fact, if you use Adobe Bridge, you don't even need to launch Photoshop!

- **Applying settings**

- **Converting images**

- **Converting from Camera Raw (Photoshop CS4)**

- **Using, or not using, Quick Fix settings**

- **Resizing images: now or later**

APPLYING SETTINGS

One handy and quick method of updating a set of RAW files is to apply Camera Raw settings without actually converting the image to a TIFF or JPEG file. Both Photoshop Elements and Photoshop make the application of Camera Raw settings to multiple files quick and easy.

Why would you want to apply settings without doing a conversion? The most common reason is to apply a set of global changes that a number of files will need, such as white balance correction, without having to apply these settings to each file as you convert it. If you have several (or several hundred) images that all need one or two common corrections in addition to individual adjustments, this is a quick way to make these changes.

Applying from File Browser

Photoshop Elements users, whether on a Macintosh or a PC, can apply settings from File Browser, which is where you'll find the Apply Camera Raw Settings command (hard to miss with a name like that!).

NOTE: Photoshop Elements Organizer doesn't include the Apply Camera Raw Settings command, so you'll need to work in File Browser for this.

To get started, open File Browser from within Elements. You'll actually need to open one RAW file in Camera Raw and make all the adjustments needed. This image will serve as the reference image that all the others will inherit settings from. Here are the steps to follow:

1. Navigate to the folder that contains the images you want to update.

2. Select the first RAW image you want to update and double-click it to launch Camera Raw.

3. Make the global changes that every image will need, such as white balance and exposure corrections.

4. Press and hold the Alt/Option key and click the Update button, as shown in **FIGURE 5.1**, to apply the changes to that image without converting it. This will save those edits and close Camera Raw, returning you to File Browser.

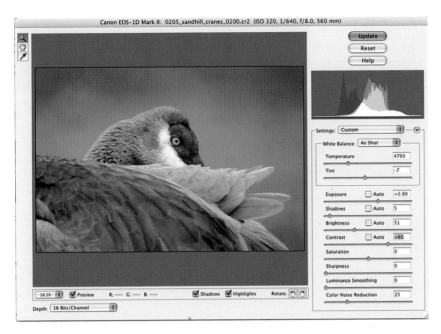

FIGURE 5.1 Holding the Alt/Option key in Camera Raw changes the buttons from Open and Cancel to Update and Reset.

5. Select the image you just updated, and then select the other RAW images you want to apply the new settings to. Use Shift+click to select contiguous files. Use Ctrl/Cmd+click to select noncontiguous files.

6. On the Macintosh, choose Automate → Apply Camera Raw Settings, which will display the dialog shown in **FIGURE 5.2**. In Windows, choose File → Apply Camera Raw Settings. The options on both platforms are identical.

7. Choose Selected Image and click Update.

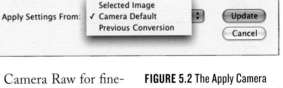

All the images you have selected in File Browser will have the settings from the first image applied to them. From here, you can either open individual images in Camera Raw for fine-tuning or move to the batch conversion step that I cover later in this chapter.

Other options in Apply Camera Raw Settings are Previous Conversion, which will update the files with the settings used in the previous conversion—useful when RAW files live in multiple directories—and Camera Raw Default, which returns the settings in the selected images to the default settings.

FIGURE 5.2 The Apply Camera Raw Settings dialog in Photoshop Elements lets you select which settings to use for updating your RAW files.

NOTE: Don't confuse Camera Default with As Shot. Selecting Camera Default will apply the settings saved as the defaults that you have when Camera Raw opens a RAW file for conversion. Whatever changes you've made through the Set Camera Default command will be applied to each image. As Shot will apply the settings used by the camera at the time of image capture.

Applying from Bridge

Bridge offers Photoshop users two ways to apply settings to multiple RAW images without converting them. If you've already made changes to one of your RAW files, start by selecting it in Bridge, then follow the steps below.

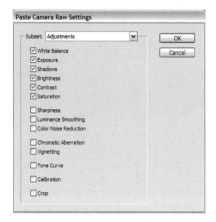

1. Choose Edit → Apply Camera Raw Settings → Copy Camera Raw Settings, or type Ctrl+Alt+C (Macintosh Cmd+Opt+C).

2. Select the other RAW images to which you want to apply the new settings. Use Shift+click to select contiguous files. Use Ctrl/Cmd+click to select noncontiguous files.

3. Choose Edit → Apply Camera Raw Settings → Paste Camera Raw Settings, or type Ctrl+Alt+V (Macintosh Cmd+Opt+V). The Paste Camera Raw Settings dialog, shown in **FIGURE 5.3**, opens and displays the options available to you.

FIGURE 5.3 Paste Camera Raw Settings lets you copy everything or just a single adjustment—the choice is all yours. I've selected the Adjustments Subset in this example.

The Paste Camera Raw Settings dialog lets you pick and choose which adjustments you want to apply. This has come in handy for me on several occasions when I've made more adjustments to an image than I want to apply everywhere. You can either click each checkbox to select or unselect the adjustment, or select a subset from the drop-down list. When you click OK, the marked adjustments will be applied to all selected images.

The other option for applying settings is similar but more direct. You'll still need to have made changes to one of the RAW images. Rather than copying and pasting settings to other images, select Edit → Apply Camera Raw Settings → Previous Conversion. This is an all-or-nothing choice; you don't have the option to select subsets or individual adjustments.

NOTE: If you're not happy with the changes, just select Edit → Apply Camera Raw Settings → Clear Camera Raw Settings to revert to the original settings.

Applying in Camera Raw (Photoshop CS4 Only)

Of all the new features in Photoshop CS4, the changes in Camera Raw to support batch processing are the most exciting to me. With this newest release, it's possible to have all your RAW files open in Camera Raw at once for easy selection and modification. As you can see in **FIGURE 5.4**, thumbnails for all selected images are displayed in a scrolling panel on the left side of the preview area.

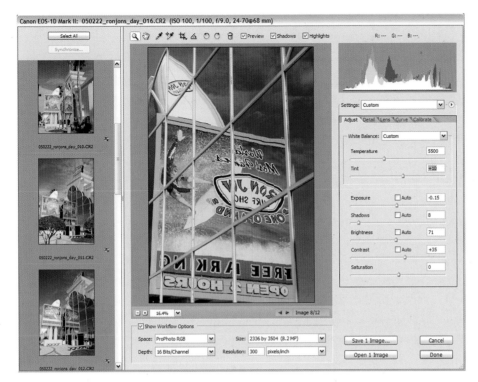

FIGURE 5.4 The new version of Camera Raw in Photoshop CS4 handles multiple files for quick and easy settings changes.

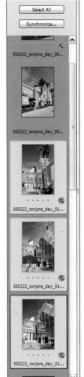

When multiple files are selected, either via Bridge or through the Photoshop File → Open menu, the Camera Raw interface changes a bit to handle the new features.

The Filmstrip, shown in **FIGURE 5.5**, displays a thumbnail for each image open in Camera Raw. Above the thumbnails are two buttons. Select All is pretty obvious. Synchronize is the button that will apply your adjustments to all selected images.

FIGURE 5.5 The Filmstrip displays all RAW files open in Camera Raw. The Synchronize button applies changes to all selected images.

NOTE: You can work on a subset of images in the Filmstrip by selecting individually, or with the Shift or Ctrl/Cmd keys and clicking for multiple files.

NOTE: You can resize the thumbnail panel by dragging the vertical separator bar between the thumbnails and the preview area. Larger thumbnails are easier to work with when making edits.

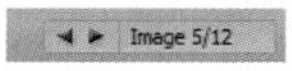

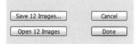

FIGURE 5.6 The navigation buttons let you move from one image to another.

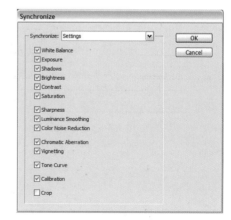

FIGURE 5.7 The Save and Open buttons change to show how many images will be affected.

Just below the preview area are navigation buttons with an image counter (**FIGURE 5.6**). This lets you move from one image to the next without selecting individual thumbnails. Finally, the buttons for Save and Open (**FIGURE 5.7**) change to reflect the number of selected files.

To apply settings from within Camera Raw, start by selecting the images in Bridge. Choose File ➔ Open in Camera Raw. If you are already in Photoshop, you can select File ➔ Open and select the files you want to modify.

There are two ways to apply changes to multiple files in Camera Raw. The first is by selecting multiple thumbnails and making the adjustments on the first image. Each adjustment you make will be applied to every selected image, and the thumbnails will update to reflect the changes.

The second method takes advantage of that Synchronize button. Select the image that you want to use for your adjustments and correct it until you have the settings you want. Now, select all the desired thumbnails and click Synchronize. The dialog box shown in **FIGURE 5.8** will open, letting you select which adjustments to apply to all images.

After selecting which settings to apply, click OK, and all selected images will be updated.

Finally, after all adjustments have been made, click the Done button to apply the changes and close Camera Raw. Alternatively you can select Save or Open. Open will launch Photoshop if it isn't already running, launch Camera Raw to apply the changes to your RAW files, and leave the selected files open for post-processing. Save does the conversion work for you and saves the files in the selected format without going into Photoshop for editing. I'll cover why you'd want to do that in just a bit.

FIGURE 5.8 The Synchronize dialog (look familiar? It should; it's the same as the Paste Camera Raw Settings dialog seen earlier) has options to apply all settings or subsets.

CONVERTING IMAGES

Of course, the end result when working with RAW files is to convert them into an actual image file, whether that is a JPEG, TIFF, PSD, or some other format that can be used directly. Converting a single image is straightforward enough: Just click the OK button or Open button in Camera Raw and all settings are applied to the image, which is then opened in Photoshop Elements or Photoshop. But, since the theme of this chapter is automating Camera Raw, let's focus on batch, or multiple file, conversions. Both Photoshop Elements and Photoshop support batch conversions, but each does it in a different way.

Converting from File Browser

Photoshop Elements handles batch conversions from within File Browser. All the processing work is done through the Process Multiple Files command, which can convert, rename, and resize your images without needing to open and save each one manually.

1. To get started, select File ➜ Browse Folders and navigate to the folder containing the RAW files you want to convert.

2. Select the RAW files you want to convert by Shift+clicking for contiguous files or Control+clicking for noncontiguous files.

3. From the File Browser menu bar on Windows choose File > Process Multiple Files. On the Macintosh, choose Automate ➜ Process Multiple Files. You'll see the dialog box shown in **FIGURE 5.9**.

For this example, I've already selected the images I want to convert, so Process Files From will be left at File Browser. If I wanted to convert an entire folder of RAW files, I'd select Folder. The Import option isn't valid for RAW images, and the Opened Files option implies that you've already converted the images and have them open in Elements.

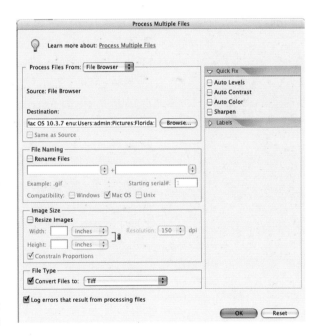

FIGURE 5.9 Process Multiple Files in the File Browser is the quickest way for Photoshop Elements users to do batch conversions.

Destination lets you navigate to the folder you want to save the converted images in. If you're converting with the Folder option, you can also specify whether to save to a new folder or save to the same folder by checking Same As Source.

File Naming has the same options as the Batch Rename dialog. Refer to chapter 1 for details on naming options and suggestions.

Image Size gives you the option of resizing your image as part of the conversion process. Unless you have a specific use intended for the converted file, I recommend not resizing during the conversion. The exception to this is when converting directly from RAW to JPEG for Web use. I occasionally convert RAW files for multiple uses by running Process Multiple Files once to save them as 16-bit TIFF files and a second time to create small JPEGs that will be used for a contact sheet. For the second pass, I select Resize Images and set a width of 320 and leave Constrain Proportions checked.

File Type has a number of options available, but for normal conversions, the one you'll want to select is TIFF. This converts your images at 16 bit (if selected in Camera Raw) for the most color information possible.

NOTE: If you convert files to JPEG, they will be saved as 8-bit images regardless of the setting in Camera Raw.

Converting from Organizer on Windows

Organizer has a very limited form of batch conversions. In fact, it really isn't a batch at all but rather an interactive way to open multiple RAW files for editing. File Browser is a much better way to convert multiple RAW images, but it can be done through Organizer if you feel the need.

1. To get started, launch Organizer by clicking Photo Browser 🔳 Photo Browser in the Photoshop Elements toolbar.

2. Select the RAW files you want to convert by Shift+clicking for contiguous files or Ctrl+clicking for noncontiguous files.

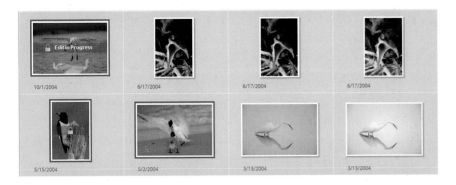

FIGURE 5.10 Organizer tracks which images are selected for conversion with a banner-and-lock icon. (Images courtesy Art Morris, www.birdsasart.com.)

3. Next choose Edit ➔ Go to Standard Edit. This will open Adobe Camera Raw with the first image. If you've already made your corrections in File Browser, just click the OK button to convert the image. Camera Raw will automatically open the next selected RAW file, continuing until all selected images have been converted. Organizer displays a lock icon over the images that are selected for conversion, as shown in **FIGURE 5.10**, and a lock with the text Edit In Progress for images that have been converted and opened in Elements.

If you haven't applied settings to the RAW files you're opening from Organizer, the quickest method is to make the adjustments to the first image and then select Previous Conversion from the Camera Raw Settings drop-down list.

NOTE: Because you'll need to OK each image in Camera Raw, and because Photoshop Elements keeps all the images open, I recommend using File Browser to do batch conversions.

The final checkbox in Process Multiple Files is Log Errors, which creates a text file list of any errors that occurred during the conversion process. I suggest leaving this option checked so that you have a reference to any possible errors. Unchecking the option will ignore any errors that occur.

CONVERTING FROM CAMERA RAW
(PHOTOSHOP CS4 ONLY)

I've already covered how to apply settings to multiple files from within the Photoshop version of Camera Raw. To perform the actual conversion, you simply need to select the files in the Filmstrip and click Save as shown in **FIGURE 5.11**.

This will display the Save Options dialog, shown in **FIGURE 5.12**, which has several settings for the converted files, including where to save, renaming the images, and what file type to convert to.

Destination options are to Save in Same Location or Save in New Location. Clicking Select Folder will automatically change the drop-down list to Save in New Location. File Naming has the same options available as the Batch Rename command, which was covered in detail in chapter 1.

FIGURE 5.11 To batch-convert the selected images in Camera Raw, click Save Images.

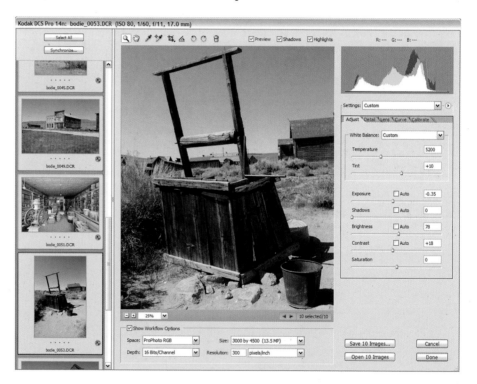

FIGURE 5.12 The Save Options dialog is where you'll specify where to put the converted files and what file type you want them converted to.

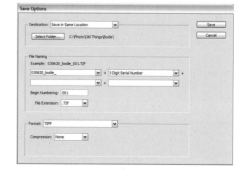

Format offers several options, including digital negative, TIFF, and JPEG. You'll typically want to save as TIFF to take full advantage of the 16-bit color space. Selecting JPEG will automatically convert your files as 8 bit regardless of the depth setting in Camera Raw. If you do select JPEG, you have the option to set quality; I recommend setting this to Maximum for best results.

Once you click Save, all images will be converted and saved in the specified location. As the images are processed, a not-very-obvious status link is displayed above the Save button (**FIGURE 5.13**). Clicking this link will open a Camera Raw Save Status dialog (**FIGURE 5.14**) showing which files have been processed and as what type. If you want to cancel the conversion, click the Stop button in this dialog.

NOTE: Holding the Alt/Option key while clicking Save bypasses the Save Options dialog. The Save Options from the previous conversion will be used if you bypass the dialog.

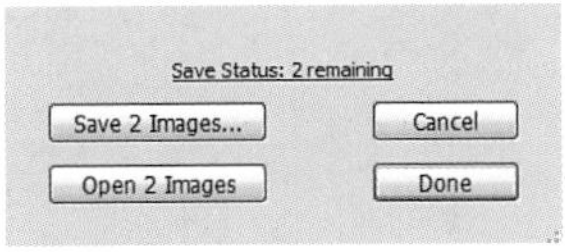

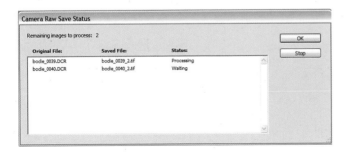

FIGURE 5.13 Camera Raw shows the number of files being converted. Clicking the link opens the Save Status dialog showing the progress of the batch conversion.

FIGURE 5.14 To cancel a batch conversion, click the Stop button in the Camera Raw Save Status dialog. This dialog also shows which files have been converted and to what file type.

USING, OR NOT USING, QUICK FIX SETTINGS

The Process Multiple Files dialog in Photoshop Elements has a nifty feature that you might be considering. The Quick Fix and Labels checkboxes on the right will apply the Auto settings and Sharpen after the image has been converted. Here's my advice on using these settings: **DON'T!** At this point, all Auto settings have been handled in Camera Raw, so there's no point in letting Elements decide to change things around. Sharpen should never be used, and certainly not at this point in the workflow.

NOTE: Don't confuse Sharpen with Unsharp Mask. Sharpen is an automatic application of the filter with no control over settings. Unsharp Mask, on the other hand, gives you full control over how your image is sharpened.

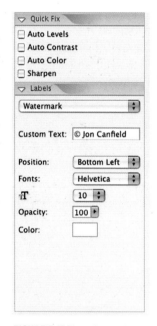

Labels is a way of placing text directly on your images. It's sort of like the date imprints from some point-and-shoot film cameras. Do you really want text plastered onto your image? The one instance in which you might want to do this is when converting images for Web use. In that case, a copyright notice might be appropriate (**FIGURE 5.15**).

To place a copyright notice, select Watermark from the drop-down list. In the Custom Text field, enter the text you want to appear in the converted image. Select a position, either Bottom Left or Bottom Right (unless you want to be bold and place your text in the center of your image), and then set the Opacity and color of your text.

NOTE: To insert the copyright symbol ©, press Opt+G (Macintosh) or Alt+0169 on the numeric pad (Windows).

FIGURE 5.15 The only time I would use the Labels option during conversion would be to place a copyright notice on an image destined for the Web.

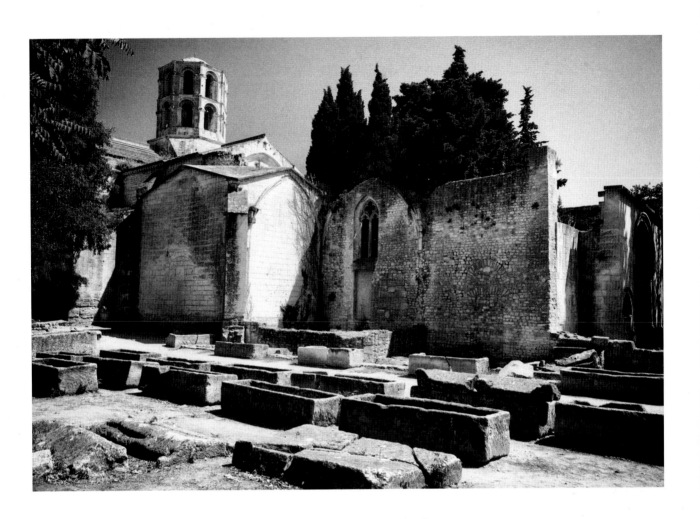

RESIZING IMAGES: NOW OR LATER

The odds of your using your image files at their native size run a close second to your winning the lottery. Almost every image you take is going to be made larger or smaller for its intended use, whether that be a print or for Web display. All Adobe Camera Raw users can automate the resizing task during the conversion process by using the appropriate options in the Process Multiple Files command. Users of Photoshop also have the option to resize in Camera Raw.

If you know in advance that you'll be using a particular image at a certain size, Camera Raw does a very good job of image resizing. **FIGURE 5.16** shows the same image resized to the same dimensions in two different programs. The image on the left was resized in Camera Raw, while the image on the right was resized in Photoshop using Bicubic Smoother.

FIGURE 5.16 *Left*: This image was resized in Camera Raw as part of the conversion process. *Right*: The same image resized in Photoshop after conversion. There is very little difference in quality between the two images.

The Photoshop version of Adobe Camera Raw includes a Size option below the preview area shown in **FIGURE 5.17**. The Size drop-down has seven preset sizes with the default being the RAW file's native size. Depending on the resolution of your camera, you'll see different options, as shown in **FIGURE 5.18**. For example, the

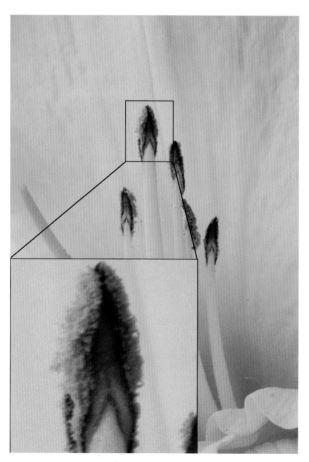
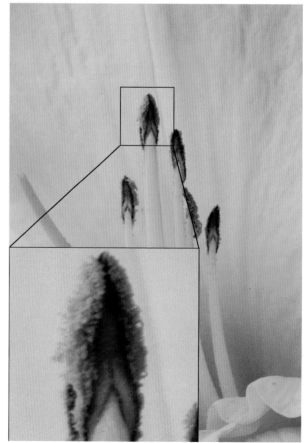

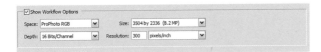

FIGURE 5.17 The Size list in Photoshop's version of Camera Raw lets you resize the image during conversion, saving a step later in the workflow.

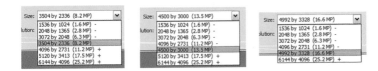

FIGURE 5.18 Depending on the resolution of your camera, the size options will vary. As shown here, the sizes are for *(left)* the 8.2 MP Canon ID Mark II, *(center)* the 13.5 MP Kodak SLR/c, and *(right)* 16.6 MP Canon IDs Mark II.

Canon 1D Mark II has seven sizes listed with three smaller, one native, and three larger; the Kodak SLR/c and Canon 1Ds Mark II have more options to reduce the file than enlarge.

As you can see, the preset size options remain nearly constant: 1.6 MP, 2.8 MP, 6.3 MP, 11.2 MP, 17.5 MP, 25.2 MP are the possible choices, although not every option will be seen with every camera. (For instance, the 17.5 MP option isn't available with the Canon 1Ds Mark II, and the 6.3 MP option won't be seen with Nikon D70 RAW files.)

For the most flexibility, I prefer to resize after the conversion. Of course, if you are using Photoshop Elements, this is the only option available to you unless you are using Process Multiple Files, which makes the decision a bit easier. I prefer to resize one time for the best possible quality. Since any resizing will resample the image, it's best to avoid multiple sizing operations when possible.

NOTE: In the case of Photoshop, I've touched on what is possible only with automation. Actions can be recorded to handle tasks such as saving in multiple formats. For even more power, Photoshop supports scripting for total control over the workflow.

SUMMARY

Whether you have two files or two thousand files that need editing, using the batch-processing features in Camera Raw, Bridge, Photoshop, and Photoshop Elements can help make the job easier and more consistent.

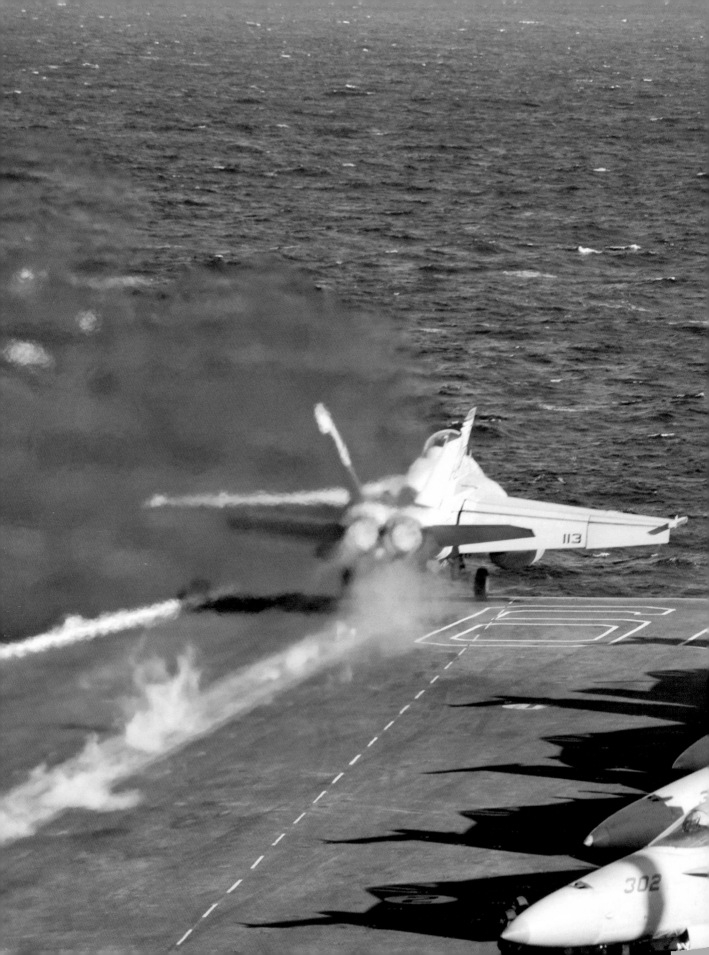

6

ADVANCED CONVERSION OPTIONS

Most of this chapter is for those using Adobe Camera Raw in Photoshop CS4. However, the sections on cropping and straightening apply to everyone. This version of Camera Raw offers many more controls over RAW image processing than does the CR in Photoshop Elements or even in earlier versions of Photoshop. Don't get me wrong—Elements and Camera Raw is a powerful combination that can handle most RAW file conversion tasks. But when you have the need for advanced controls, or you are processing hundreds or thousands of RAW files on a regular basis, you'll quickly appreciate the extra features found here.

- **Fixing chromatic aberration**

- **Adjusting vignetting**

- **Using the Curves control**

- **Calibrating Camera Raw**

- **Cropping and straightening**

- **Creating custom settings**

- **Saving in Camera Raw**

FIXING CHROMATIC ABERRATION

Chromatic aberration is that color fringing, or colored halos, seen on some images, particularly in high-contrast areas of the image. (See **FIGURE 6.1** for an example.) It's more problematic with zoom lenses and is made worse by the sensitivity of digital sensors. Chromatic aberration occurs when all of the light wavelengths coming through the lens don't align precisely at the same point, in this case the sensor in your camera.

Camera Raw has two sliders located on the Lens tab (**FIGURE 6.2**) to help correct chromatic aberration. Chromatic Aberration R/C adjusts red/cyan fringing problems, while Chromatic Aberration B/Y adjusts blue/yellow fringing problems. Both controls work by adjusting the amount of red and blue compared to the amount of green.

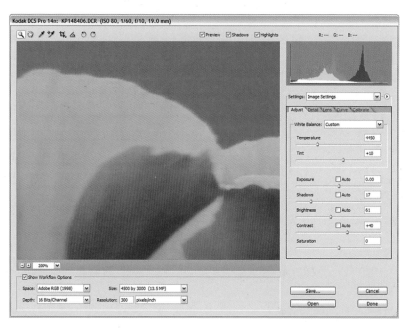

FIGURE 6.1 Chromatic aberration rears its ugly head as color fringing most noticeable around high-contrast areas of the image.

FIGURE 6.2 The adjustment sliders for Chromatic Aberration are located on the Lens tab of Camera Raw. Separate sliders control red/cyan and blue/yellow color fringing.

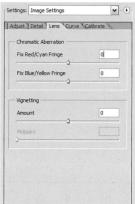

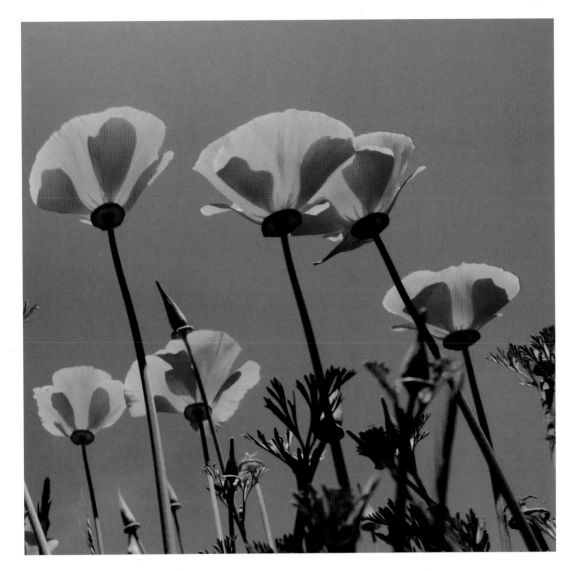

FIGURE 6.3 The original image shows strong chromatic aberration on the edges of the flowers. This is easy to correct in Camera Raw.

If you're wondering why only the red and blue are adjusted, remember that photo sites have red, blue, and green filters. The Chromatic Aberration sliders work by adjusting the strength of the reds and blues or by adding or subtracting those colors. Enough with the theory—how about a real example? The image of California poppies (**FIGURE 6.3**) shows strong chromatic aberration along the edges of the flower petals.

To start, open the image in Camera Raw and make any major adjustments, such as in exposure, shadows, contrast. To help with your adjustments, turn Sharpening off in the Detail tab. This will make it easier to tell what is actually chromatic aberration and what is an artifact of sharpening.

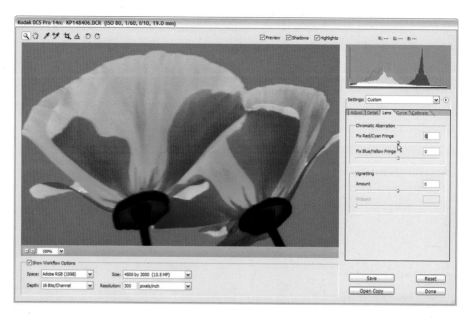

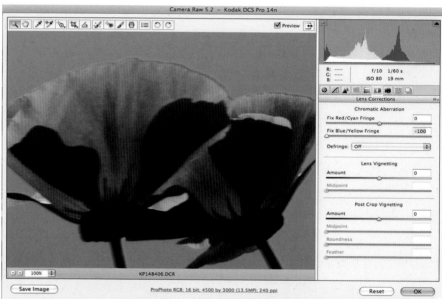

FIGURE 6.4 *Top*: Holding down the Alt/Option key while clicking the Fix Red/Cyan Fringe hides the Blue channel and shows that this image has no fringing problems that need correcting in this channel. *Bottom*: The same Alt/Option-click combination on Fix Blue/Yellow Fringe shows strong chromatic aberration along the edges of the flower petals.

By holding down the Alt/Option key while clicking each of the Chromatic Aberration sliders, you can hide the other color channel to make it easier to see where the problem areas are. In **FIGURE 6.4**, there is an obvious problem in the Blue channel while the red/cyan channel looks fine.

Don't be afraid to drag these sliders large amounts if needed. Unlike adjustments to noise, there is little, if any, image degradation or softening when using the

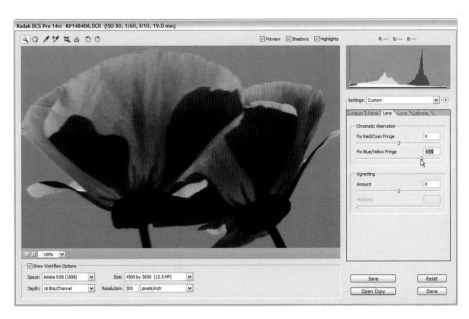

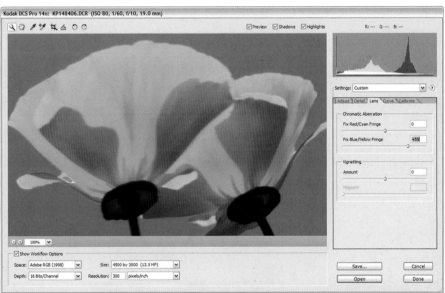

FIGURE 6.5 *Top*: A fairly large adjustment of +55 to the Fix Blue/Yellow Fringe slider has reduced the color fringing in this image to an acceptable amount. *Bottom*: The adjusted image with all color channels visible shows a much cleaner edge along the flower petals.

Chromatic Aberration controls. The image shown in **FIGURE 6.5** needed to have a +55 adjustment to the Fix Blue/Yellow Fringe slider to correct the fringing problems.

On its own, it may be hard to see what has changed. A side-by-side comparison of the image shows greatly improved definition between flowers and sky. **FIGURE 6.6** shows the original along with the corrected image.

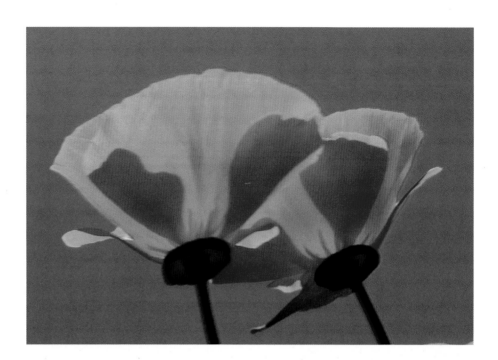

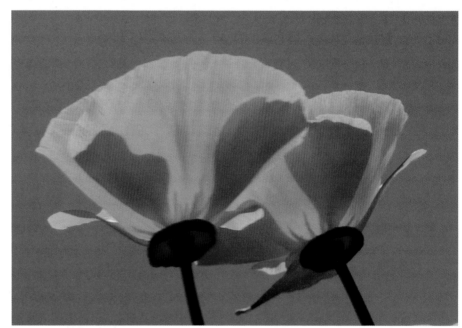

FIGURE 6.6 *Top*: Before correcting chromatic aberration, the image has color fringing along the edges of the flowers. *Bottom*: After the correction there is much better definition between flower and sky.

ADJUSTING VIGNETTING

Vignetting, or darkening of the edges, is a fairly uncommon problem for most digital cameras. It occurs when the light hitting the edge of the sensor isn't as strong as the light hitting toward the center, and it's more likely to occur at wide apertures and with full-frame sensors, such as the Kodak Pro SLR and Canon 1Ds.

Correcting Vignetting

The control is located in the Lens tab, just below the Chromatic Aberration sliders (**FIGURE 6.7**), and has two adjustments—Amount and Midpoint. Amount controls how much lightening is added to the corners of the image, while Midpoint controls how wide of an area is affected by the controls.

FIGURE 6.8 shows a typical example of vignetting in a RAW file. It's most obvious in the upper corners of the image as a darkening of the sky. To correct this, you need to adjust the Amount slider to the right.

Increasing the Amount slider to 45 removed the darkening so that the sky now has an even tone from edge to edge (**FIGURE 6.9**).

The default setting for the Midpoint slider is 50. Lowering the slider by moving it to the left will apply the Amount adjustment to a larger area of the image. Increasing the value by adjusting to the right reduces the area affected by the Amount adjustment. **FIGURE 6.10** shows the difference between the two settings. Your goal is to keep all changes to a minimum, only adding enough Amount and Midpoint adjustment to reduce the vignetting to an acceptable amount.

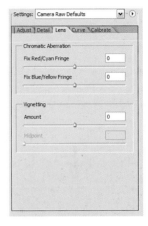

FIGURE 6.7 The Vignetting controls are found on the Lens tab. Sliders control the Amount and Midpoint of the adjustment. Unless the Amount is set to a value other than 0, the Midpoint slider is disabled.

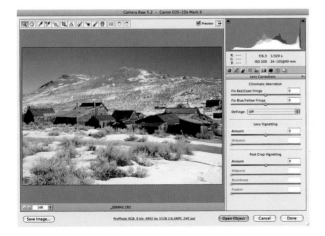

FIGURE 6.8 A typical vignetting problem. The corners of this image are a little darker than the rest of the image and can be adjusted with the Amount slider of the Vignetting control in Camera Raw.

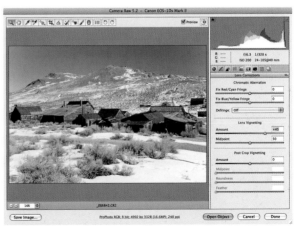

FIGURE 6.9 Adjusting the Amount slider to 45 eliminated the vignetting in this image.

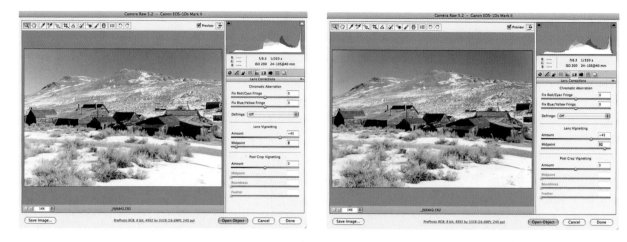

FIGURE 6.10 *Left*: Adjusting the Midpoint to the left increases the area affected by the Amount adjustment. *Right*: Higher Midpoint adjustments confine the Amount adjustment to a smaller area.

You may not be able to completely correct vignetting in the RAW file without making the image unacceptably light. A little experimentation will give you an idea of how much correction a particular image can handle. The final image, after levels and cropping in Photoshop, is shown in **FIGURE 6.11**.

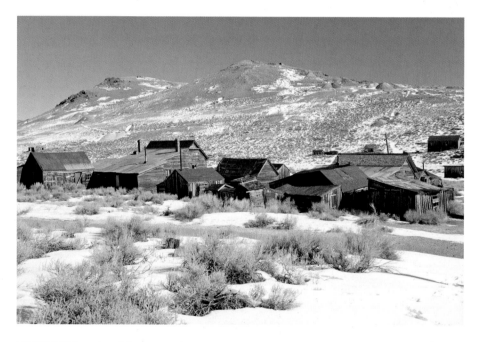

FIGURE 6.11 The end result has corrected all vignetting that was seen in the original image without affecting the remainder of the image.

Getting Creative: Adding Vignetting

Vignetting correction doesn't always have to be about removing it. A creative technique to add an old feel or to draw the viewer's attention to the middle of an image is to add vignetting to it. This can be done in Photoshop as well by using a graduated fill adjustment layer, but it's much simpler to do it in Camera Raw with the Vignetting control.

The image used in this example is from Bodie, California (**FIGURE 6.12**). I had to shoot through glass and, as you can see from the color version, this didn't help the image. With a "can't hurt a broken image" mentality, a little experimentation with grayscale and vignetting seemed to be in order!

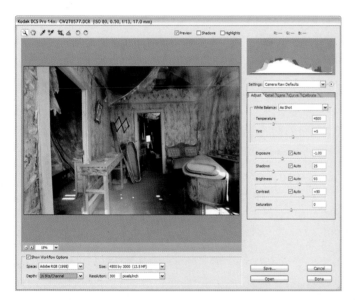

FIGURE 6.12 The RAW image is unusable as is. The glare and reflections from shooting through an old window have made this image a candidate for either creative editing or the trash can.

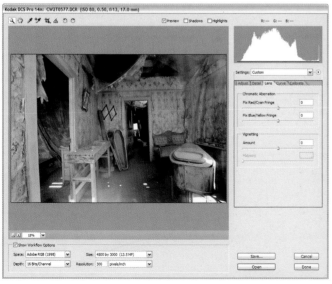

FIGURE 6.13 Desaturating the image and making adjustments to the Calibration sliders gives the image a good black-and-white feel that looks quite a bit better than the original.

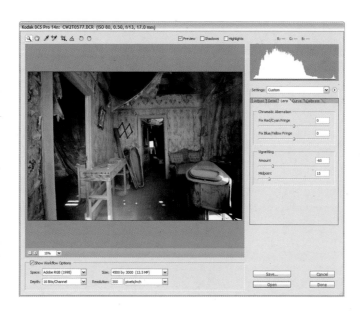

FIGURE 6.14 After adjusting the Vignetting Amount and Midpoint sliders to darken the corners, the image is looking more aged.

To start with, I reduced Saturation on the Adjustments tab in Camera Raw to –100. This technique was covered in chapter 4, Beyond the Basics. This made the reflections less visible and already improved the image. Adjusting the Calibration sliders to +100 Blue Saturation, +100 Blue Hue, –25 Red Hue, and –39 Red Saturation, and boosting the shadow tint a little resulted in the image shown in **FIGURE 6.13**.

Next, on the Lens tab I wanted to darken the edges to give it a vignetted look similar to the images that come out of many old cameras. A setting of –60 with a Midpoint lowered to 15 looked right for this example (**FIGURE 6.14**). The image is now ready for conversion, so I clicked Open.

The final step was to give the image a nice sepia tone. For this, select Image > Adjustments ➔ Photo Filter and select Sepia from the Filter list, as shown in **FIGURE 6.15**. Increasing the Density, or strength of the filter—in this case, to 57%—gives the image its final toning, with the end result shown in **FIGURE 6.16**. Digital lemonade from a digital lemon!

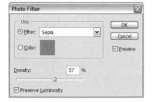

FIGURE 6.15 The Sepia Photo Filter is selected to give the image a toned look.

NOTE: For full information on black-and-white conversions from Camera Raw, see chapter 4.

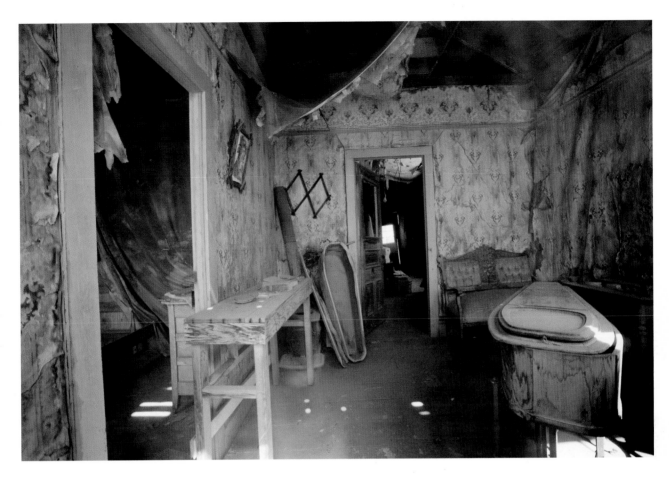

FIGURE 6.16 The finished image has taken advantage of the problems in the original RAW file to create a photo that looks old.

USING THE CURVES CONTROL

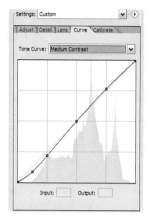

FIGURE 6.17 The Curves control in Camera Raw can fine-tune adjustments to shadow, highlight, and mid-tone areas.

If the adjustments made with exposure, brightness, shadows, and contrast on the Adjust tab aren't quite what you want, the next stop will be the Curves tab, shown in **FIGURE 6.17**. The Tone Curve drop-down includes four preset options:

Linear: No additional contrast adjustment is performed on the RAW file prior to conversion. This is the method used by the Photoshop CS/Photoshop Elements 3 version of Camera Raw.

Medium Contrast: This is the default setting for Camera Raw. It adds a little bit of contrast and is well suited to most RAW images.

Strong Contrast: This adds more contrast to the RAW image. It works for some images, particularly those with strong bold lines, but is not a good choice for portraits or softer images.

Custom: You can add and move points along the curve to create your own contrast settings. Any adjustment from the three other presets on the Curve will automatically change the setting to Custom. Up to fourteen points can be created.

The Curves control shows a tone curve over a histogram of image data. The tone curve is used to adjust the image shadow, highlight, and mid-tones in a precise manner, similar to the way Curves works in Photoshop. The real power of using Curves in Camera Raw is that you are making these changes on the RAW data, giving you more latitude with any adjustments made. If you use Curves in Camera Raw, be sure that Highlights and Shadows checkboxes are selected to help you avoid clipping.

As with the Curves control in Photoshop, upper right is highlight data and lower left is shadow data. Raising the tone curve by dragging it up from the current position will lighten the pixels in that color range. Dragging the line down will darken the corresponding pixels.

White point and black point can also be changed by dragging the vertical lines to the start of image data on the histogram. Dragging the left line sets the black point, while dragging the right line will set the white point.

To clear a point from the tone curve, drag it off the control.

NOTE: To select a specific tonal value, hold down the Ctrl/Cmd key while moving the mouse over the preview area. The tone curve will show where that color value is on the curve. Clicking will place a point on the curve at that value.

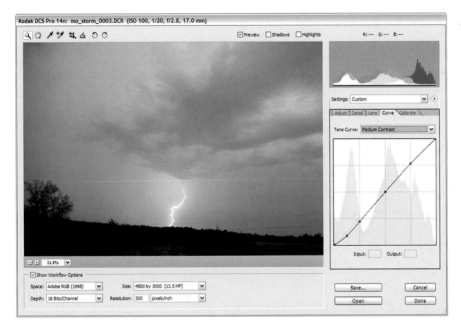

FIGURE 6.18 The clouds in this image don't have the menacing look I remember from taking the image. Even after making adjustments to exposure, shadows, and contrast, I want to fine-tune the image.

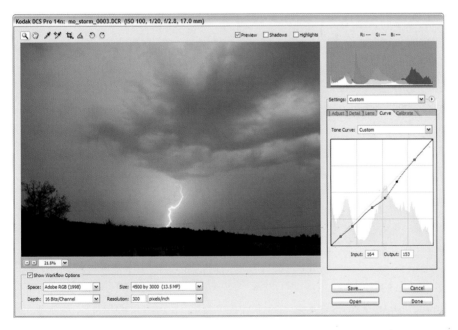

FIGURE 6.19 Adjustments to the tone curve give the clouds much more impact without affecting the rest of the image.

The image shown in **FIGURE 6.18** is close to what I want but still a little flat, especially in the clouds. To adjust the image, I want to modify the curve to darken the mid-tones with more control than the Adjust tab gives me.

Holding down the Ctrl/Cmd key while moving the mouse pointer over the image preview area will cause a dot to display on the curve that corresponds to that color value. This makes it easy to select exactly the points on the tone curve to adjust. The main area of adjustment is in the mid-tones, which I've darkened by dragging the points below the line, as shown in **FIGURE 6.19**.

CALIBRATING CAMERA RAW

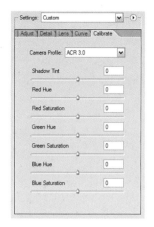

Camera Raw can be calibrated, or adjusted, to match unique lighting situations or, if you're really having problems, your individual camera. The controls on the Calibrate tab, shown in **FIGURE 6.20**, make it possible to adjust the saturation and hue of each color channel as well as the shadow tint.

Depending on your camera model and version of Photoshop, the Camera Profile list may contain any or all of the following choices:

> Embedded: the profile contained in the RAW file.
> ACR 4.5: the profile that was provided with the Photoshop CS3/Photoshop Elements 6 and 7 version of Adobe Camera Raw.
> ACR 5.0: the built-in profile included with the Photoshop CS4 version of Camera Raw.

FIGURE 6.20 The Calibrate tab in Camera Raw enables you to correct for color casts in an image or for your specific camera.

Adjusting Shadow Tint

Adjustments to color temperature and tint will sometimes create a color cast in the shadow areas of your image. The Shadow Tint slider is used to correct this problem. Although it varies depending on the color cast, the slider usually adds green when moving left, or negative, and magenta when moving right, or positive. **FIGURE 6.21** shows both of these adjustments.

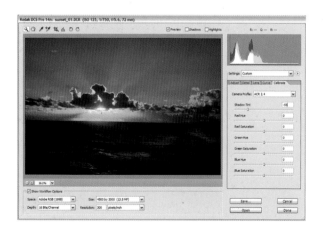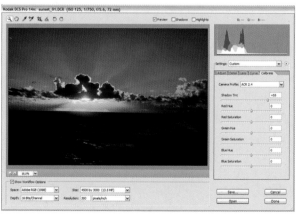

FIGURE 6.21 *Left*: The Shadow Tint slider corrects color casts that can be created when adjusting the Temperature and Tint controls. Negative numbers typically add green. *Right*: Positive numbers add magenta to the shadows.

Adjusting Hue and Saturation

In chapter 4, and earlier in this chapter, I used the Hue and Saturation sliders on the Calibrate tab to adjust black-and-white images. A more common use for these controls is to correct color images, removing any color cast from each of the channels that may be present in your RAW captures.

I suggest adjusting hue first and modifying saturation only if needed.

Use the Hue and Saturation sliders to adjust the red, green, and blue in the image. Look at the preview image as you make adjustments until the image looks correct to you. Moving the Hue slider to the left (negative value) is like a counter-clockwise move on the color wheel, and moving it to the right (positive value) is like a clockwise move. Moving the Saturation slider to the left (negative value) desaturates the color, and moving it to the right (positive value) increases saturation. **FIGURE 6.22** shows an image from the Badlands that needs some calibration help. Colors are flat, with too much red, and the green hue is off.

After making adjustments, the image, as seen in **FIGURE 6.23**, is much more accurate in color. Since this particular camera tends to have a similar problem with landscape-type photos in overcast lighting, you may have noticed that I've saved the settings to reuse for other similar images. I'll cover saving settings later in this chapter.

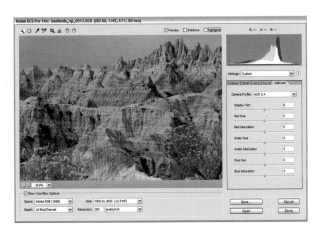

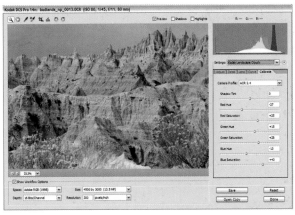

FIGURE 6.22 This image needs some calibration help. All three colors are off, with too much red and green and not enough blue.

FIGURE 6.23 After adjustments to the Hue and Saturation sliders, the color in the image is much more accurate than it was in the original RAW image file.

CROPPING AND STRAIGHTENING

Cropping and straightening in Camera Raw have two main advantages over doing the same operations after conversion: First, it's one less step to perform later. Second, it reduces the file size of the open image. And when you are looking at file sizes of up to 95 MB (in the case of a Canon 1Ds Mark II converted to 16-bit TIFF), the file size savings can be well worth the time spent to crop in Camera Raw.

Camera Raw offers two tools for cropping. The first is the conventional Crop tool ⬚, which works just like the Crop tool found in Photoshop's toolbar. The second is the Straighten tool ⬚, which crops your image while rotating it to straighten a horizon or other line in the image.

> **NOTE:** If the image is too small after cropping, you can use the Size control to resize the image prior to conversion. The Size list box will show the current size with the selected crop area.

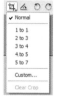

FIGURE 6.24 The Crop tool can make life easier for you when it comes to resizing your image for a specific output need.

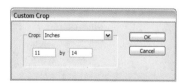

FIGURE 6.25 The Custom Crop option makes it possible to create cropping presets that fit your needs.

The Crop Tool

Cropping is pretty straightforward: You drag a selection rectangle around the part of the image you want to keep. If that was really all there was to cropping, it wouldn't be worth discussing here, though, would it?

The Crop tool hides some helpful goodies behind its drop-down menu, as shown in **FIGURE 6.24**. To access the menu, click and hold the mouse button on the Crop tool until it displays.

By default, there are six options available. Normal is a freeform crop: Whatever you drag out on the preview is what you'll get with no resizing applied to the converted image. The other options are all aspect ratios: 1 to 1 is square, 4 to 5 is 25 percent longer in length or width than the other dimension, etc. Like Normal, these choices don't resize the image on conversion, but they do ensure that when you resize in Photoshop, the dimensions will fit into these standard formats.

Custom is where you can save some time and effort if you know in advance that you'll be using a RAW file for a particular use. For example, when you select Custom, the dialog box shown in **FIGURE 6.25** is displayed.

Clicking the Crop drop-down list allows you to select the type of crop you want to create: Ratio, which is what the presets use, or a specific size in pixels, inches, or centimeters (**FIGURE 6.26**). These final three choices will all resize the image to match the dimensions you select for the custom crop.

For this example, I've created a custom crop of 11 × 14 inches. Once the custom crop is created, it will be listed in the drop-down menu for the Crop tool (**FIGURE 6.27**).

NOTE: If you create a custom crop, it will be selected in the drop-down menu by default.

With this 11 × 14 crop selected, any area that I drag out with the Crop tool on the Preview window will be automatically sized to 11 × 14 inches when converted. To reflect this, the Workflow Options area of Camera Raw is updated to show the crop size rather than the dimensions in pixels (**FIGURE 6.28**).

After dragging out a cropping selection, you can modify the crop by dragging the handles in the corners of the selection. Moving the mouse pointer over the selection handle displays a double-ended pointer 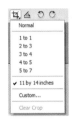. Any resize will keep the same dimensions (if anything other than Normal is selected from the menu). Moving the mouse pointer just outside the handles will show a curved arrow pointer that lets you rotate the selected crop, as shown in **FIGURE 6.29**.

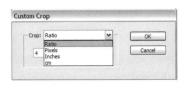

FIGURE 6.26 You can either create a new crop based on ratio like the presets or a custom size crop that will resize the image on conversion.

FIGURE 6.27 The custom crop you create will be displayed in the drop-down menu for the Crop tool.

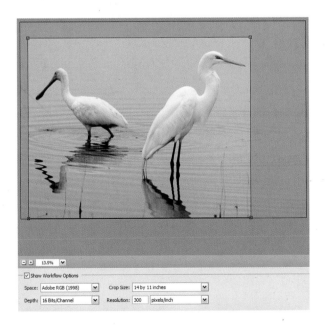

FIGURE 6.28 When you use a custom crop for a specific size, the Workflow area of Camera Raw updates to show Crop size rather than pixel dimensions.

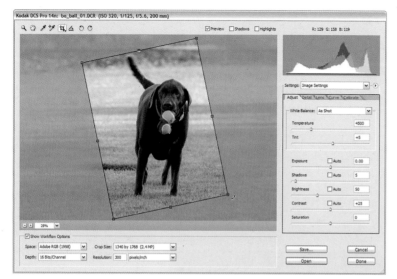

NOTE: The Rotate tool is similar to the Straighten tool, covered next, with one exception: It changes only the rotation of the crop, not the size of the selection.

When the crop selection is rotated and opened in Photoshop, the image is rotated to match the angle shown in Camera Raw (**FIGURE 6.30**).

FIGURE 6.29 Using the Rotate tool to correct a tilt or to just get creative.

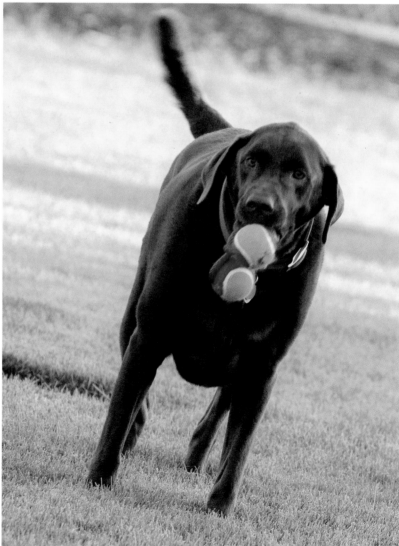

FIGURE 6.30 After the RAW file is converted, it will be rotated to match the crop lines in Camera Raw.

The Straighten Tool

The Straighten tool ⊿ is a shortcut to correcting horizons or other angle problems in the RAW file. The tool can be used either horizontally or vertically and will always create a crop that is as large as possible for the corrected image.

To use the Straighten tool, begin with a crooked image (kind of makes sense doesn't it?) and find a reference in the image that should be straight. Click and drag out a line, as shown in **FIGURE 6.31**.

The length of the line doesn't matter; the crop will always be as large as possible given the angle of the line. When you release the mouse button, the image will be cropped and rotated as shown in **FIGURE 6.32**.

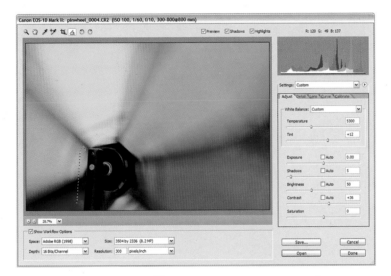

FIGURE 6.31 Drag out a line with the Straighten tool after finding a reference in the image that should be straight.

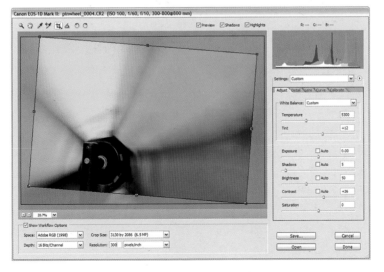

FIGURE 6.32 After the mouse button is released, a crop will be created that is as large as possible with the selected angle.

CREATING CUSTOM SETTINGS

Unlike the version of Camera Raw included with Photoshop Elements 6 or 7, Camera Raw users in Photoshop CS4 have options available to them when it comes to saving custom settings for use with other images. The options to create custom settings are located in the pop-up menu next to the Settings drop-down list (**FIGURE 6.33**).

Depending on the option selected in Preferences (**FIGURE 6.34**), settings will be saved as an XMP "sidecar" file or within the Camera Raw database. I strongly recommend using the XMP sidecar option. This way, if you move images or if the Camera Raw database becomes corrupted for some reason, you still have all of your settings.

NOTE: XMP files are just formatted text files that contain the settings information you select.

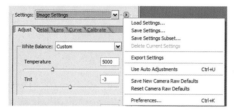

FIGURE 6.33 All of the custom settings options are located in the pop-up menu next to the Settings list.

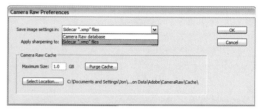

FIGURE 6.34 The Camera Raw Preferences dialog lets you select whether to store settings in a separate XMP file or in the Camera Raw database.

Changing Camera Raw Defaults

Selecting Save New Camera Raw Defaults updates all settings and makes them the default for any new image opened in Camera Raw. This option works exactly like the one in the Photoshop Elements version of Camera Raw. If you find yourself constantly making the same changes to your RAW files before converting them, such as the default bit depth, or turning Auto settings on or off, changing the defaults in this way makes sense. That isn't usually the case, though, which makes the other options more attractive and useful.

Saving Settings

Rather than changing the default for all images opened in Camera Raw, selecting Save Settings accomplishes a very similar task but with more flexibility. Save Settings lets you create new named sets of defaults, making it quick and easy to apply several changes at once to an image. This can be very useful when shooting under controlled lighting situations in which you might have custom white balance and tint settings but don't want to make these adjustments each time.

Saving Subsets

Save Settings Subset, shown in **FIGURE 6.35**, is the perfect way to create groups of settings for special situations. Earlier in the chapter, I showed an example of modifying the Hue and Saturation sliders in the Calibrate tab. Since this particular camera always needs a similar adjustment for the same lighting situation, I saved the Calibrate settings as a subset named Kodak Landscape Cloudy. The Subset drop-down list has quick-selection options for each of the control sets in Camera Raw. Alternatively, you can click and choose which settings you want to save.

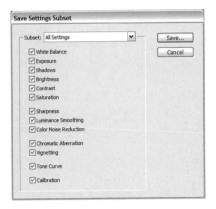

FIGURE 6.35 Save Settings Subset is a great way to create special groups of settings for reuse.

Other Settings Menu Options

Load Settings opens a standard File Open dialog. If you save your settings files to the default location, you won't need to use this option, as the custom settings will show up in the Settings drop-down list. If you've saved the file somewhere else, use Load Settings to find the .XMP file and open it.

Delete Current Settings removes the active custom setting. To use Delete Current Settings, select the custom setting in the Settings drop-down menu to activate it, and then select Delete Current Settings. This will remove the .XMP file, so use it with care!

Export Settings will move settings from the Camera Raw database to an external .XMP file. If you've set your preferences to save to .XMP, as I recommended earlier, this command won't be needed.

Use Auto Adjustments will toggle the Auto Adjustment settings on the Adjust tab on or off depending on their current state. If you've saved Camera Raw Defaults to turn Auto Adjustments off, this is a quick way to restore them for a RAW file. The Auto Adjustment settings also control how Bridge displays RAW thumbnails. Reset Camera Raw Defaults will restore all settings to their original state. If things get too hairy, sometimes it's best to just start over.

SAVING IN CAMERA RAW

Available in Camera Raw with Photoshop CS4 is the ability to save converted files without actually opening them in Photoshop. Although it's most useful when converting multiple images, selecting Save rather than Open can be a quick way to do the basic conversion work now while saving the post-processing tasks for later. For detailed information on using Save, refer to chapter 5, Automating Camera Raw.

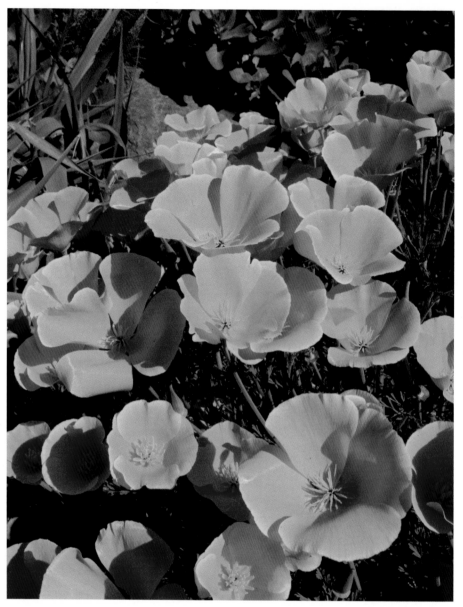

before

SUMMARY

The advanced version of Camera Raw contains a number of additional features geared toward the pro or high-volume shooter. It will also appeal to anyone who likes to tweak settings to get an image just right. (Hello, my name is Jon, and I'm a tweaker.) All of these options are designed to give you the highest quality image possible before conversion, with the least amount of effort required after the conversion. Still, there are some things that are best left until later, and I'll cover those in the next chapter.

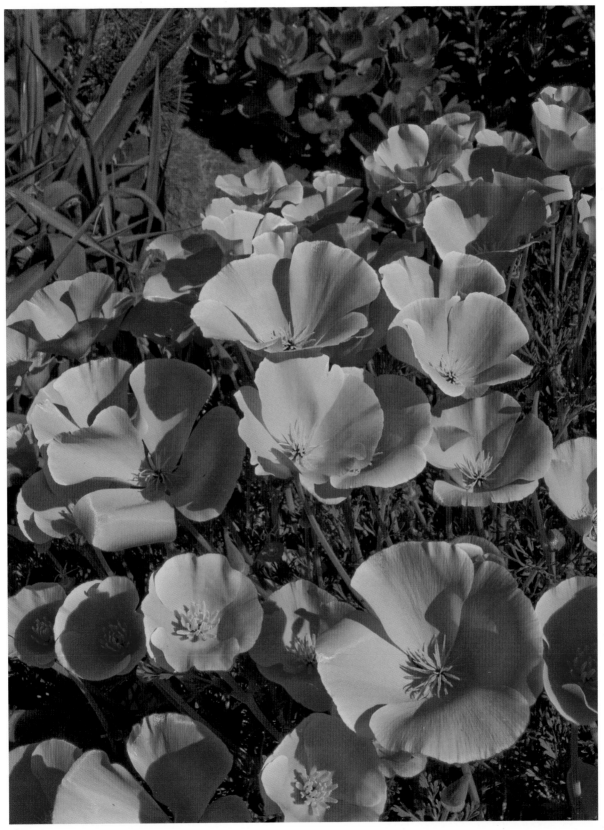

after

FINISHING TOUCHES

RAW is a fantastic way to capture images and retain a high level of control over how the image is processed. As good as RAW is, there are still some things that are either better left to post-conversion or only possible after conversion. This final chapter will take a look at some of the most important post-conversion edits that help put the final polish on your images.

- **Adjusting output levels**

- **Dust removal**

- **Increasing dynamic range**

- **HDR (Photoshop CS4 only)**

- **Resizing**

- **Sharpening**

- **Saving as TIFF**

- **Saving as JPEG**

ADJUSTING OUTPUT LEVELS

Making a Levels adjustment after converting the RAW image might seem odd and, in fact, shouldn't be necessary with proper adjustment in Camera Raw. (Refer to chapter 3 for details on adjusting exposure, shadows, brightness, and contrast.)

But the Levels control is useful for making adjustments to *output* levels, particularly for printing situations in which the printer can't match the shadow and highlight detail of the screen image. By adjusting the slider below the levels graph, you modify the black point and white point for the output device. As with all image edits, I recommend using adjustment layers whenever possible to avoid changing the master image. To adjust output levels, Layer → New Adjustment Layer → Levels. For most inkjet printers, I recommend setting the Output Levels shadow slider at 10 to prevent shadow detail from blocking up and the highlight slider to 240 to avoid clipping in the highlights, as shown in **FIGURE 7.1**. This slightly reduces the contrast in your image and prevents blank areas in the highlights that may look odd due to the paper color, since areas with a value of 255 have no ink and let the paper show through.

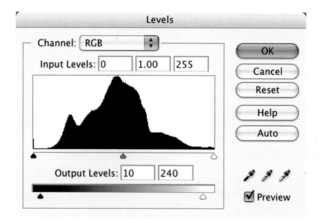

FIGURE 7.1 Adjust the output shadow and highlight sliders at the bottom to 10 and 240, respectively, to avoid clipping with most ink jet printers.

DUST REMOVAL

Anyone who uses a digital SLR and more than one lens will have problems with dust on images. Note that I say *will*. There is no way around it, although some cameras, such as the Sony Alpha, have hardware features to reduce the problem.

When you view your images in Camera Raw, the telltale dark spots, more obvious in areas with little or no detail, such as sky, are sure signs of dust on the sensor. While you can't eliminate them in Camera Raw before conversion, Photoshop Elements and Photoshop have two tools that help clean them up after the conversion.

Spot Healing Brush: This is usually the best method of cleaning up dust. Select a brush size from the Options bar that is close to the size of the dust spot and leave Type set to Proximity Match. When you click on the dust spot, Photoshop will replace the area under the brush with color values that match the surrounding area.

Clone Brush: When the dust bunnies are too big, or you find what looks like a hair in your image, the Clone brush may be your best bet. This tool works by sampling an area of the image and duplicating it as you paint with the tool.

NOTE: The Healing Brush is a cross between the Spot Healing and Clone brushes. It works by sampling an area, like Clone, but uses the sampled pixels to blend with the existing ones rather than a direct replacement of the pixels. I recommend using Spot Healing whenever possible.

INCREASING DYNAMIC RANGE

If you've recently switched from print film to digital, you have probably realized that digital images don't have the same dynamic range, or ability to capture detail from shadow to highlight, as do film negatives. Where negative film can record as much as eight stops of light or more, digital is closer to transparency film with a range of about five stops.

There are two ways to increase the dynamic range in your digital images. The first is to use two copies of the same image with one adjusted for shadow detail and the other for highlights in Camera Raw, combining them in Photoshop Elements or Photoshop after the conversion. The second method is to capture two or more images of the same scene with different exposure settings and combine them after conversion, also in either version of Photoshop. The steps for both methods are essentially the same, so I'll use the more common situation—having one image to work with. (I won't tell you how long it took me to begin taking multiple exposures at different settings. Let's just say that I learned how to work with one image for this technique.)

To create an expanded-range image from the same exposure, open the RAW file in Camera Raw. (**FIGURE 7.2** shows the starting point for this example.) With Shadow and Highlight clipping enabled, the blue and red show that details are being clipped at both ends of the image. The first conversion will be optimized for shadow detail. Using the Alt/Option key while adjusting the Exposure slider, raise the exposure by moving it to the right until no clipping is seen in the preview area (**FIGURE 7.3**). At this point, the highlights are going to be totally blown out, but don't worry about that for now.

FIGURE 7.2 Here's the original image. Fixing the shadows will blow out the highlights, and adjusting for the highlights will cause the shadows to go black.

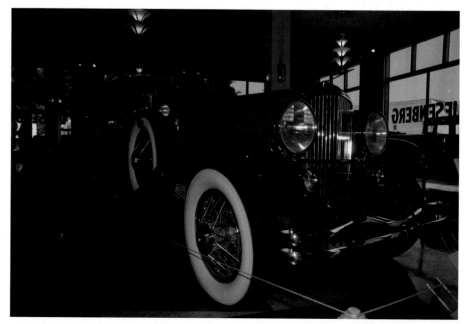

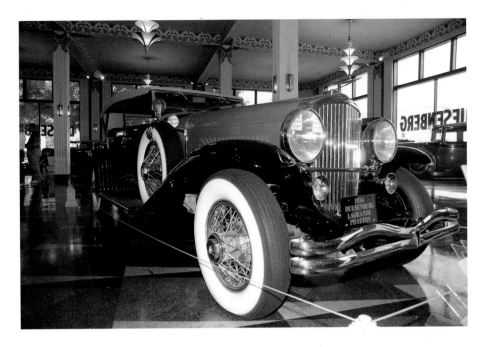

FIGURE 7.3 The first copy of the RAW file is optimized for shadow detail before conversion. The clipped highlights will be corrected in the second copy.

Make corrections to Blacks, Brightness, and Contrast, as shown in **FIGURE 7.4**, and then convert the image by clicking OK (Photoshop Elements) or Open (Photoshop).

NOTE: Photoshop Elements users must convert the image to 8 bit for these techniques. Choose Image → Mode → Convert to 8 Bits/Channel if you converted as a 16-bit file.

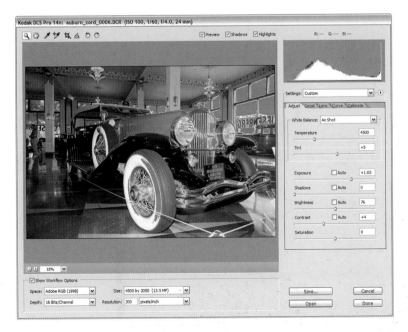

FIGURE 7.4 Make all additional adjustments in Camera Raw to get the maximum shadow detail possible.

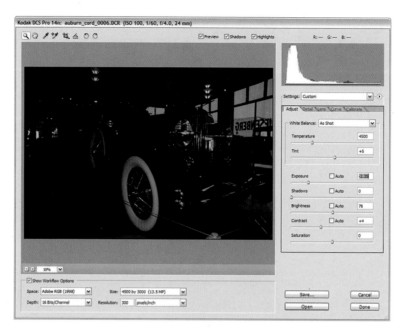

FIGURE 7.5 The second copy of the RAW file is optimized for highlights. Lost shadow detail isn't a concern here; it will be recovered when the images are combined.

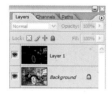

FIGURE 7.6 The Layers palette shows both versions of the file and is now ready for optimizing.

The second copy of the RAW image will be optimized for highlight detail. Open the same image in Camera Raw and, using the Alt/Option key technique described above, drag the Exposure slider to the left until highlight clipping is eliminated. Once again, the image will show clipping, this time in the shadows. And, once again, ignore the clipping because you are only worried about highlight detail in this copy of the image.

After you make corrections to shadows, brightness, and contrast, the image will look like **FIGURE 7.5**. Convert the image with the OK or Open buttons.

1. Now the fun and magic start. Select the window with the darker of the two images and choose Edit ➔ Select All (Ctrl/Cmd+A), then Edit ➔ Copy (Ctrl/Cmd+C).

2. Now select the window with the lighter image and choose Edit ➔ Paste (Ctrl/Cmd+V). If you look at the Layers palette, you'll see two layers (**FIGURE 7.6**). The Background is the lighter image, and Layer 1 is the darker image.

NOTE: You can close the darker image to free up memory. All edits will be done on the combined image.

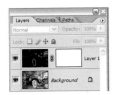

FIGURE 7.7 After a layer mask is added, a white rectangle is shown next to the thumbnail for Layer I.

At this point, the two programs differ. Photoshop Elements users should skip down to the Step 3 that follows **FIGURE 7.10**.

3. The next step for Photoshop users is to add a layer mask to Layer 1. With Layer 1 selected in the Layers palette, click the Layer Mask icon at the bottom of the palette. Layer 1 will then have a white rectangle next to the thumbnail, as seen in **FIGURE 7.7**.

4. Select the Background in the Layers palette and copy it with Select ➜ All and Edit ➜ Copy.

5. Press the Alt/Option key and click the white rectangle in Layer 1. The image looks like **FIGURE 7.8**.

6. Select Edit ➜ Paste. Both the layer mask icon and the image window will have a black-and-white version of your image, as seen in **FIGURE 7.9**.

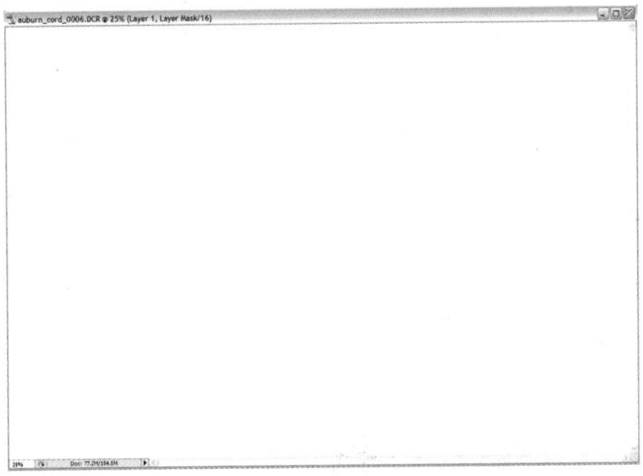

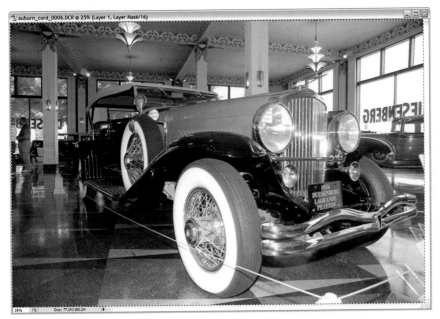

FIGURE 7.8 After you copy the Background and selecting the layer mask, the image will be all white.

FIGURE 7.9 After you paste the Background into the layer mask, a black-and-white version of the image will be displayed.

7. For the final step, select Filter ➔ Blur ➔ Gaussian Blur, and select a radius of 30. (This is personal preference, but I find that 30 is a good starting point and works for many images. Some images may need much less or quite a bit more. You'll need to experiment to see what the right level is for the image you're working on.) Select the Background, and your image will look like **FIGURE 7.10**.

Photoshop Elements doesn't have layer masks, so combining images takes quite a bit more work. Steps 1 and 2 are the same as the Photoshop method. In Elements, you need to erase dark areas of the image to reveal the highlights. By changing the opacity of the eraser, some of the dark will be left, building density in the image.

What follows picks up for Photoshop Elements users where Step 2 left off.

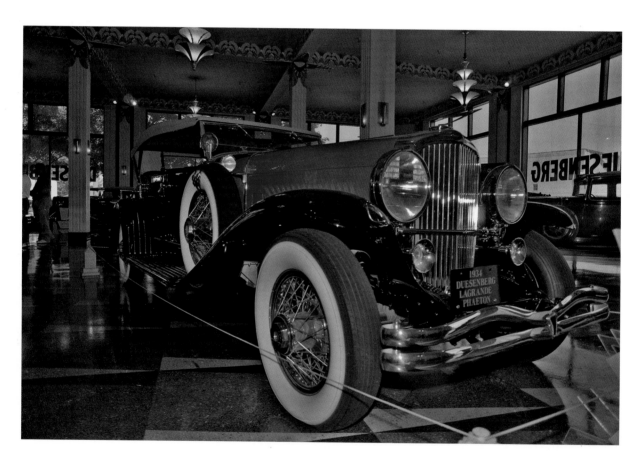

FIGURE 7.10 After a Gaussian Blur has been applied and the Background selected, the combined image shows a much wider dynamic range than the original images.

3. After copying the dark image to a new layer of the light image, make sure Layer 1 is selected in the Layers palette.

4. Select the Eraser tool and lower the Opacity to 45% in the Options bar. Select a brush size that will work with the area you want to erase, and erase the areas you want to restore light detail.

NOTE: Alternatively, you can use the Selection Brush or Magic Wand to create a selection before using the Eraser tool. This will confine any erasing to the selected area. Select the area of your image that you want to modify and then make your edits. The final result takes a steady hand but can allow you to create an image with much better dynamic range (**FIGURE 7.11**).

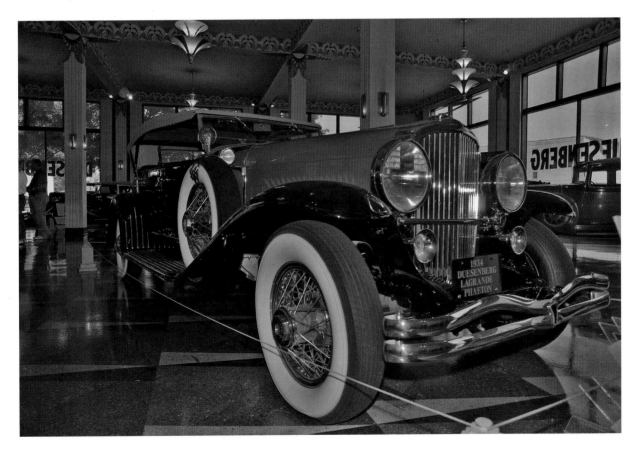

FIGURE 7.11 The final image after editing in Elements has a wider dynamic range than the original images.

HDR (PHOTOSHOP CS4 ONLY)

Photoshop CS4 has a feature known as High Dynamic Range, which makes the process of merging multiple images easier but does require more preparation when shooting. To get the most from HDR, you need to shoot at least three images, and often as many as seven, depending on the dynamic range in the scene. Each of these images is captured at a different exposure. I recommend using Aperture Priority to keep a fixed depth of field and changing the shutter speed. Each exposure should be one stop apart, and for decent results your camera needs to be on a tripod with nothing in the scene moving.

Selecting File ➔ Automate ➔ Merge to HDR will let you select the images and then create a high-dynamic-range image that contains all the detail possible. The files are 32 bit and must be converted for printing or other use.

RESIZING

Back in chapter 5, I covered how to resize images using the Photoshop CS4 version of Camera Raw during the conversion process, and in chapter 6 when using the Crop tool. If you remember from that discussion, I suggested not resizing during the conversion unless you had a specific use for the converted image.

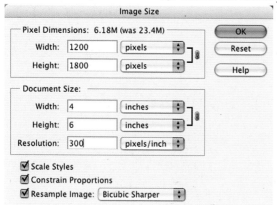

Most images don't fall into this category, though, so you'll most likely find yourself resizing in Photoshop Elements or Photoshop. Both applications use the same method and dialog, shown in **FIGURE 7.12**.

To access this dialog, choose Image ➔ Resize ➔ Image Size (Photoshop Elements) or Image ➔ Image Size (Photoshop).

For printing, enter the width or height in the Document Size fields for the final print. For Web or screen use, enter a width or height in the Pixel Dimensions fields.

FIGURE 7.12 Image Size is used after the conversion to resize an image file for a specific use.

NOTE: If you leave Constrain Proportions checked—and I recommend that you do to avoid distorting the image—set the important dimension, either width or height. The other dimension will be set automatically.

Resample Image offers several options. For photographic images, there are only three options that will give good results.

> **Bicubic** is the standard method and does a good job for most images.

> **Bicubic Smoother** is the best choice when *enlarging* images and will do the best job of interpolation when adding pixels to create a larger image.

> **Bicubic Sharper** is a good choice when *reducing* image size. This option can oversharpen an image, though, so if the resized photo appears too sharp, use standard Bicubic.

SHARPENING

Back in chapter 3, I discussed sharpening in Camera Raw and recommended that you wait until all image edits and resizing are done before applying any sharpening to your converted RAW files.

Unsharp Mask

Photoshop Elements and Photoshop offer several options to sharpen images, all of which are found under Filters ➜ Sharpen. The only one that I recommend using, though, is Unsharp Mask. This filter gives you complete control over how your images are sharpened and can be adjusted for different needs.

FIGURE 7.13 *Left:* Before the application of Unsharp Mask, the image doesn't display strong contrast between edges. *Right:* After Unsharp Mask, the edges are more defined, giving the appearance of sharpness.

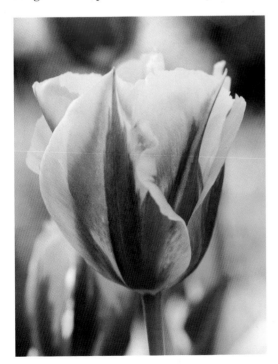 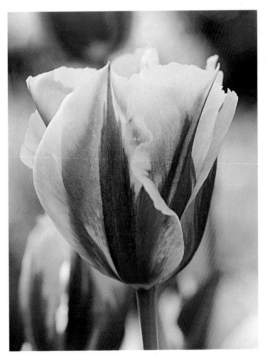

The name Unsharp Mask might sound a bit odd. After all, you want to sharpen the image, not unsharpen it, right? Unsharp Mask works by increasing the contrast along edges in your image, as shown in **FIGURE 7.13**, increasing the appearance of sharpness. Don't think of this as a magic tool, though—it isn't going to make an out-of-focus photo look sharp, but it will make your images look more defined by increasing the contrast around the edges.

Unsharp Mask offers three controls for determining how the image is sharpened:

> Amount determines the strength of the contrast added to the edges. Images with high levels of detail will typically use a higher Amount setting of 150 percent or more.

> Radius determines how wide the halos will be that are added to the edges to enhance the contrast. Radius is the most critical setting in Unsharp Mask and will have lower numbers, usually under 1.0 for high-detail images and higher numbers for lower detail subjects.

> Threshold controls how much difference there must be between pixels before they are considered edges. High-detail images will use lower settings here, because you want more of the image to have defined edges. Values in the 0 to 4 range are common here. Portraits, on the other hand, will have large areas that you don't want to sharpen, such as skin tones, so you'll use a higher Threshold setting, with 8 or more being common.

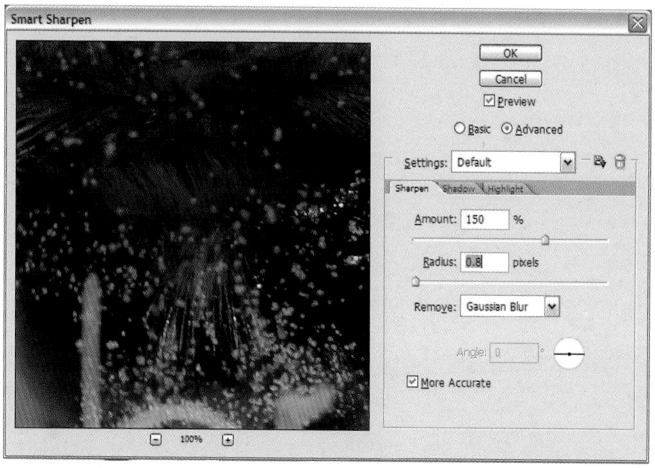

FIGURE 7.14 The Smart Sharpen filter includes a number of features that make it a useful alternative to Unsharp Mask.

Smart Sharpen

Photoshop users also have the Smart Sharpen filter. Selecting Filters → Sharpen → Smart Sharpen gives you access to this new filter (**FIGURE 7.14**), which has the benefit of more control over how the image is sharpened. Photoshop Elements users will find this under Enhance → Adjust Sharpness. Using the new controls in Smart Sharpen, you can adjust how shadows and highlights are affected as well as how blurring is reduced in your image.

By default, Smart Sharpening starts in Basic mode, which has controls for Amount and Radius that work in the same way as the Amount and Radius controls in Unsharp Mask. The new feature in Basic mode is Blur Removal. Clicking on the Remove list box shows three options:

> **Gaussian Blur** is the default and uses the same method as Unsharp Mask.

> **Lens Blur** is the most useful for photographs and controls how edges and textures are detected to maintain higher detail in those areas.

> **Motion Blur** is the third option and is used to control the angle of correction. Selecting Motion Blur will activate the Angle control. This setting is most effective for images that have a small amount of camera or subject movement.

The Advanced option adds Shadow and Highlight tabs to the dialog. Both tabs work in an identical manner on their respective areas and have three controls:

> **Fade Amount** controls how much the sharpening should be reduced in the shadows or highlights. Zero is no reduction at all, while 100 will have the effect completely removed from the shadows or highlights.

> **Tonal Width** determines how wide of a range of tones will be affected by sharpening. Lower numbers will remove the sharpening effect from only the darkest or lightest areas, while a higher number affects a wider range of tones. In general, I suggest keeping this slider at or below 50 for both shadows and highlights.

> **Radius** works in a similar manner to the Radius slider on the Sharpen tab, but rather than looking for contrast between edges, it determines how wide of an area to use when deciding what the shadow or highlight area is.

I suggest using the More Accurate setting for best results. It does increase the amount of time needed to apply sharpening to the image, but the end result is worth the time.

Finally, if you find yourself frequently using the same adjustments, you can save them for future use by clicking the disc icon next to the Settings list.

SAVING AS TIFF

When all your efforts to produce the ultimate image from your RAW image are done, you'll obviously want to save your changes. Saving as a TIFF file will give you the most flexibility and retain all of the quality contained in your image. If you do your edits with adjustment layers (and I recommend you do so), saving as a TIFF file will retain the layers, making adjustments for other uses later much easier.

NOTE: Why not PSD? At one point, PSD was the only way to save files with layers. Now that TIFF supports layers, I recommend saving as TIFF for wider compatibility with other applications and future compatibility if the PSD format changes.

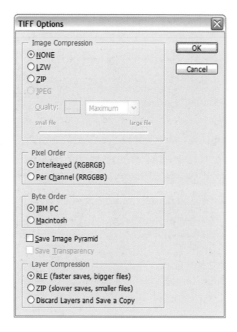

FIGURE 7.15 The TIFF Options dialog offers a number of settings for your file, including compression and layers.

After selecting TIFF as the file type, the Options dialog offers several choices, as shown in **FIGURE 7.15**.

Image Compression can reduce the size of the saved TIFF file—helpful when you're working with 16-bit files and saving with layers. LZW offers the most compatibility between applications that support TIFF, but still there are some commonly used programs that will not be able to read files that have LZW compression. I recommend not using JPEG compression because it is a "lossy" format, or one that throws away information from the image, reducing image quality. ZIP uses the compression format popular on Windows computers and will generally result in the smallest TIFF file but have more compatibility problems. For the best compatibility, select NONE, which will result in the largest file sizes but can be read by any program that opens TIFF files.

Byte Order doesn't really matter these days. If you use a Windows computer, select IBM PC. Macintosh users should select Macintosh. This option defaults to the platform you are working on and was more of an issue in the earlier days. Macintosh and Windows write bytes in the opposite order of each other, and although this used to be a problem going from one platform to another, most programs now understand both orders.

Save Image Pyramid and Save Transparency are used by other programs to take advantage of special features in the TIFF file. Image Pyramid provides multi-resolution information, useful for some applications such as page layout programs that can use a lower resolution version of the image. Transparency saves the additional information, or alpha channel, for use in other programs. Elements and Photoshop always use the highest resolution image and retain transparency.

Layer Compression will compress data for each layer rather than having to flatten the image. These options will be available only if the image contains multiple layers. RLE will generate the largest size but opens much faster than ZIP. The final choice will flatten your image and save a copy.

SAVING AS JPEG

Saving your image as JPEG implies two things. First, you're willing to save with 8 bits of information rather than 16 bits. Second, you're willing to throw away some image information because saving as JPEG will reduce the file size by throwing out info. The more compression, the more you lose.

For saving your master files for archiving, I recommend using TIFF. For Web or screen display though, JPEG is the file format of choice. For Web use, I suggest using a setting of 7 or 8 as a good compromise between file size and image quality (**FIGURE 7.16**). For Format Options, Baseline is the standard method. Progressive can be useful for websites because it displays the image in multiple passes, filling in detail with each pass. The Size option will estimate the file size after saving and show an estimate of how long it will take to download.

The other option for JPEG is Save For Web (File ➜ Save For Web). Save For Web gives you a side-by-side preview of the image before and after compression and also lets you resize images (**FIGURE 7.17**). Save For Web is designed to work with files that are sized for screen use. Trying to use Save For Web with a full-size image may give you a warning message about low memory and slow performance. I've never had Photoshop crash because of this, but when they say slow performance, they mean it! If you see this message when selecting Save For Web, click No and resize the image. Alternatively, just use Save As and select JPEG.

As with the standard JPEG save dialog, a setting of 70 or 80 will give you a good compromise between image size and quality.

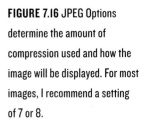

FIGURE 7.16 JPEG Options determine the amount of compression used and how the image will be displayed. For most images, I recommend a setting of 7 or 8.

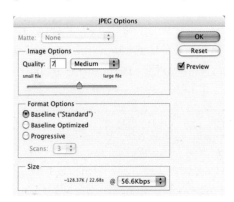

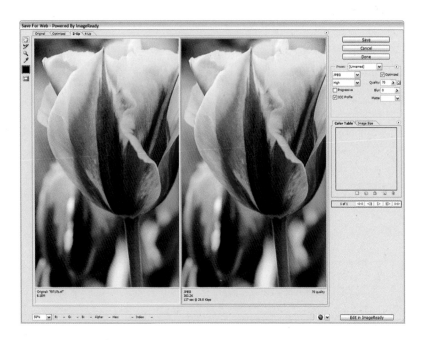

FIGURE 7.17 Save For Web offers a number of features for saving as JPEG, including the option to resize images and see a before and after preview.

NOTE: By default, Save For Web removes any profile associated with the image. If you want to retain your profile, be sure to check the ICC Profile checkbox.

One advantage (or disadvantage, depending on your point of view) is that Save For Web strips out all EXIF metadata from the file. If you don't want someone knowing what camera you used, or the settings, this will get rid of them for you.

SUMMARY

Throughout this book I've shown you ways to get the most from your digital captures by using the RAW file format. I hope the journey was a fun and educational one and that you're excited to get out and start shooting in RAW to see how much more you can wring out of your digital photos.

Photography is all about creativity for many of us, and by shooting in RAW, you extend your creative control even further. I hope you'll give RAW a try and see how it can help your images.

APPENDIX

KEYBOARD SHORTCUTS

SHORTCUT	ELEMENTS	PHOTOSHOP CS4
Alt	Enable Open Copy, Reset Controls	Enable Open Copy, Reset Controls
Alt-drag Slider	Display Clipping	Display Clipping
Tab	Next Control	Next Control
Shift+Tab	Previous Control	Previous Control
Escape	Exit Camera Raw. With Crop Tool active, Clear Crop	Exit Camera Raw. With Crop Tool active, Clear Crop
Enter/Return	Open Image	Open Image
Z	Zoom Tool	Zoom Tool
H	Hand Tool	Hand Tool
I	White Balance Tool	White Balance Tool
S		Color Sampler Tool
C	Crop Tool	Crop Tool
A	Straighten Tool	Straighten Tool
B		Spot Removal Tool
E	Red Eye Removal Tool	Red Eye Removal Tool
K		Adjustment Brush Tool
G		Graduated Filter Tool
Control/Commad+K	Open Preferences	Open Preferences
L	Rotate Left	Rotate Left
R	Rotate Right	Rotate Right
Control/Command+[	Rotate Left	Rotate Left
Control/Command+]	Rotate Right	Rotate Right
P	Toggle Preview	Toggle Preview
F	Toggle Full Screen	Toggle Full Screen
Alt/Option+Exposure Slider	Show Highlights Clipping	Show Highlights Clipping
Alt/Option+Blacks Slider	Show Shadow Clipping	Show Shadow Clipping

SHORTCUT	ELEMENTS	PHOTOSHOP CS4
U	Toggle Shadows Clipping Preview	Toggle Shadows Clipping Preview
O	Toggle Highlight Clipping Preview	Toggle Highlight Clipping Preview
Control/Command++	Zoom In	Zoom In
Control/Command--	Zoom Out	Zoom Out
Control/Command+0	Fit Preview to Window	Fit Preview to Window
Control/Comand+Alt/Option+0	Zoom to 100%	Zoom to 100%
Delete/Backspace	When Crop Tool selected, clear crop	When Crop Tool selected, clear crop. In Curves Tab, deletes selected point on Curve
Arrow Keys	Adjust Selected Control	Adjust Selected Control. In Curve tab, adjusts selected curve point
Control/Command +Z	Undo/Redo Last	Undo/Redo Last
Control/Command+Alt/Option+Z	Undo Multiple	Undo Multiple
Control/Command+Shift+Z	Redo Multiple	Redo Multiple
Control+Tab		Select Next Point in Curve
D		Deselect Point in Curve

SHORTCUT	LIGHTROOM 2.1
Control/Command+U	Auto Tone
V	Convert to Grayscale
Control/Command+Shift+U	Auto White Balance
Control/Command+E	Edit in Photoshop
Control/Command+N	New Snapshot
Control/Command+'	Create Virtual Copy
Control/Command+[	Rotate Left
Control/Command+]	Rotate Right
1-5	Set Ratings
Shift+1-5	Set Ratings Move to Next Photo
6-9	Set Color Labels
Shift+6-9	Set Color Labels Move to Next Photo
Control/Command+C	Copy Develop Settings
Control/Command+V	Paste Develop Settings
Control/Command+Return	Enter Quick Slideshow
Control/Command+P	Print Selected Photos
Control/Command+Shift+P	Page Setup
Control/Command+Left Arrow	Previous Photo
Control/Command+Right Arrow	Next Photo
Tab	Hide Panels
Shift+Tab	Hide All Panels
T	Hide/Show Toolbar
F	Cycle Screen Modes
Control/Command+Alt/Option+F	Normal Screen Mode
L	Cycle Lights Out Modes
Control/Command+Alt/Option+Up Arrow	Go to Previous Module
Control/Command+I	Hide/Show Info Overlay
I	Cycle Info Overlay
Control/Command+J	Develop View Options
R	Crop
N	Spot Removal
M	Graduated Filter
K	Adjustment Brush
D	Loupe View
Y	Before After Side by Side
Alt/Option+Y	Before After Above and Below
B	Add to Collection
Control/Command+B	Show Collection
Control/Command+Shift+B	Clear Collection

INDEX